To Rich Weisenfeld

Happiness is building your own

H.H. "Dynamite" Payson

GO BUILD YOUR OWN BOAT!

GO BUILD
YOUR OWN BOAT!

Harold H. "Dynamite" Payson

VNR VAN NOSTRAND REINHOLD COMPANY
New York Cincinnati Toronto London Melbourne

Copyright © 1983 by Van Nostrand Reinhold Co. Inc.
Library of Congress Catalog Card Number 82-25612
ISBN 0-442-24868-7

Printed in the United States of America

Designed by Bernard Stone

Published by Van Nostrand Reinhold Company Inc.
135 West 50th Street
New York, New York 10020

Van Nostrand Reinhold
480 Latrobe Street
Melbourne, Victoria 3000, Australia

Van Nostrand Reinhold Company Limited
Molly Millars Lane
Wokingham, Berkshire RG11 2PY, England

16 15 14 13 12 11 10 9 8 7 6 5 4 3 2 1

Library of Congress Cataloging in Publication Data

Payson, Harold H.
  Go build your own boat!

  Includes index.
  1. Boat-building.   I. Title.
VM321.P3 1983   623.8'2023   82-25612
ISBN 0-442-24868-7

Unless otherwise noted, all photographs were taken by Jeff
Julian and are provided courtesy of *WoodenBoat* magazine.

Dedication

Dedicated to the memory of my mother
Ethel Mae (Perry) Payson,
and to my Perry seafaring heritage.
Without it this book could
have been about raising potatoes.

Acknowledgments

To my friend Frank O'Brien,
who, with only the help of my old half-model
and my somewhat faded memory,
did an outstanding job of illustrating these pages.

To my wife, Amy,
for her help and support in so many ways.

To Bill Prosser,
for his many hours of editing.

To Jeff Julian,
for his patience and skill photographing the building
of the Gloucester Light Dory and
to *WoodenBoat* magazine for
generously allowing the use.

To Peter Spectre,
for his part in this project
and for his faith and trust in me
over the years.

To all my friends who were so supportive
in the writing of this book.
Their combined talents
and advice made it all possible.

FOREWORD

Harold H. "Dynamite" Payson was still wearing boy-size fisherman's boots when he began wrestling some of the least forgiving of our coastal waters for his livelihood. He started out with borrowed or bargain boats—skiffs, aging dories, and tired peapods, some of which came close to drowning him. By the time he decided to build his own lobster boat from scratch, he commanded a veteran's store of first-hand knowledge about the ways of boats in good weather and bad, all of it solidly learned the hard way.

To borrow one of his favorite phrases, he had another thing going for him. Working under the critical eye of his master-carpenter father, he had become skilled in the use of tools. But the elder Payson distrusted the sea, and he sawed his son's earliest ocean-going effort to bits before Dynamite had even got it wet—possibly a wise move, his son admits in retrospect, but one that meant Dynamite would have to look beyond his father's shop for guidance in marine construction. Turning his habit of close and unobtrusive observation into an advantage, he began to salt away the words and practices of the older generation of boatbuilders around him.

Among these men was Dynamite's father-in-law, Archie Rackliff. From this gentleman—in response to a request for the use of the molds from which the older man fashioned his own successful hulls—he received the shrewdest possible gift. It took the form of an untypically curt refusal:

"Go build your own boat!" Archie told him.

"It was a blessing in disguise," Dynamite says today. "But at the time, the disguise was perfect."

So—like his father-in-law—he too designed and built his own boat the hard way.

He recommends that you do the same. But with one very important difference—that with this book, you too have "another thing going for you." Here is the scrupulously honest record of setback and satisfaction, of failure and success through the scores of years and the hundreds of hulls that have measured Dynamite's life to this date.

Into the pages of *Go Build Your Own Boat!*, Dynamite has poured this wealth of highly practical experience. The first of its three sections details a time-tested method, using a lift model, of designing, lofting, and constructing a conventionally planked round-bottom hull. The second section explores the uses and misuses of plywood. In this discussion he presents a step-by-step procedure for building a light rowing dory to a classic design by naval architect Philip Bolger, and follows it up with another design from the same source—a most unusual V-bottom sailing craft that both extends the range of possible design with plywood and defines the limits beyond which it should not be pushed.

The third section is a miscellany of solutions to problems every builder in wood is certain to face, no matter what the design or method of construction—basics that have rarely been treated in such detail in the literature of small-boat work, and in some cases have never been treated at all.

One thing is sure: nowhere in this book will you find any of the boating world's truisms and clichés piously repeated—frequently without the test of real use—in all too many how-to-do-it treatises. Dynamite writes from depths of knowledge, not only of tools and techniques but also of wood itself. As he says:

"A properly sharpened hand plane almost whistles while it works; the long continuous shaving and the whistle blend together, and the plane—to me, at least—sounds happy with what it is doing.

"If that sounds a little odd to you, be advised that, to a workman, his tools develop personalities. Their curious little noises are a part of the communication between man and tool, a private language which, when understood, confirms the feel of harmony that can somehow link together the man, the tool, and the wood."

And in the following pages, Dynamite will also tell you exactly how to sharpen that plane blade.

—*Bill Prosser*

CONTENTS

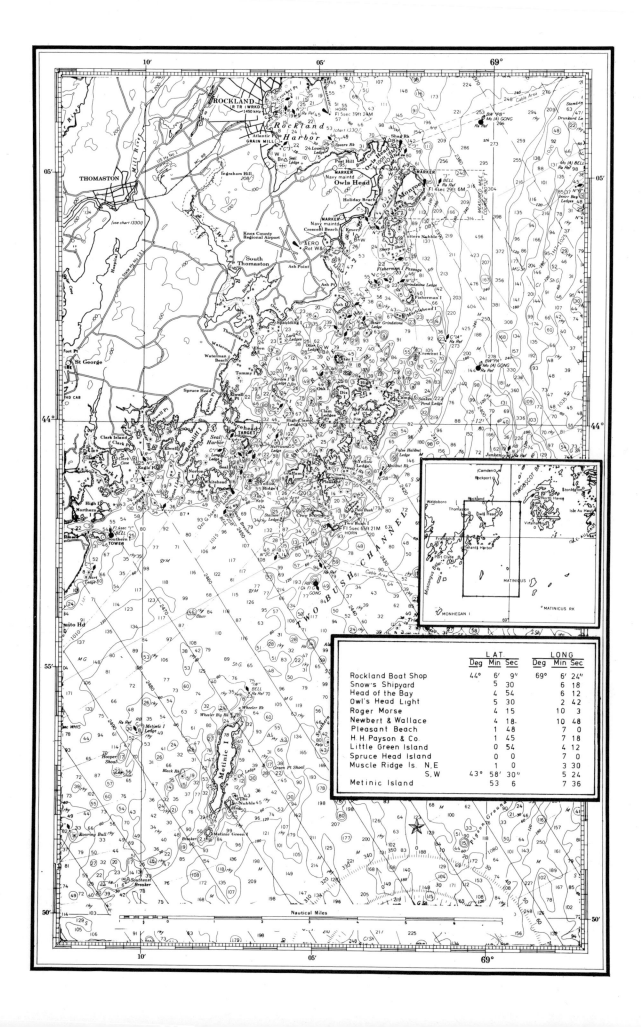

	LAT			LONG		
	Deg	Min	Sec	Deg	Min	Sec
Rockland Boat Shop	44°	6'	9"	69°	6'	24"
Snow's Shipyard		5	30		6	18
Head of the Bay		4	54		6	12
Owl's Head Light		5	30		2	42
Roger Morse		4	15		10	3
Newbert & Wallace		4	18.		10	48
Pleasant Beach		1	48		7	0
H. H. Payson & Co.		1	45		7	18
Little Green Island		0	54		4	12
Spruce Head Island		0	0		7	0
Muscle Ridge Is. N.E		1	0		3	30
S. W	43°	58'	30"		5	24
Metinic Island		53	6		7	36

Nautical Miles

GO BUILD YOUR OWN BOAT!

PART ONE

BUILDING TO YOUR OWN DESIGN

2

1 Learning Boats

When I was twelve years old, I knew exactly what I wanted to do—catch lobsters, build boats, and spend a hitch in the U.S. Navy.

You didn't have to look far to find the sources of these aspirations in the little fishing village of Owls Head, Maine, at the head of the bay where I grew up. To the north lay Snow's Shipyard, which had turned out many a coastal schooner before my time, and back in the 1940s was building wooden minesweepers for the Navy. To the east and along the north shore there were good lobster grounds, where my older friends and their fathers made a hard but adequate living hauling traps in everything from skiffs to full-size lobster boats with inboard engines. In the deep water off nearby Munroe Island, destroyers and battleships steamed through their shakedown paces and speed trials across a measured mile.

I was too young for the Navy, so I made do with taking a crack at lobstering. With neither boat nor traps, however, getting started was a real hurdle. No one in my family was a fisherman, or had anything to do with the sea. In fact, my father, who was a farmer, took a saw to the first boat I ever built before it even got wet, with the aim of keeping me from drowning. Maybe he did.

Luck, and money from picking blueberries, put me in business. I bought a leaky old Banks dory from Arthur Marriner of Ash Point for five dollars, and a dozen or so lobster pots from Lawson Small's reject pile for a quarter apiece. The pots needed a lath or two, but at the price I wasn't kicking. The lobstering license at that time was either free or maybe a buck, so for a total investment of ten dollars from my blueberry capital I was a lobsterman, and happy as a clam at high water.

A pair of eight-foot oars—what we called "an ash breeze"—got me to the fishing grounds, running from the spindle ledge below the shipyard and over to Cooper's Beach on the north shore of Owls Head.

There was a lot I liked about fishing out of that dory. On calm days she rowed easily enough, and with her narrow, flat bottom and flared topsides she would heel over right to the gunwale and no farther, allowing me—with my 128 pounds, boots and all—to snap a trap over the side without any great effort. Windy days were a different story. Then it was rowing three lengths ahead and being set five lengths back, and getting blown all over the place.

After a while, my dory began to come apart faster than I could put it back together. One season ended with no boat in the water and a dozen traps waiting to be brought ashore.

I had always heard that the double-ended, round-bottom boat of the type known as a "peapod" was the most seaworthy you could ever be in. To me, with my boyish habit of seeing everything as either black or white, that meant you could do anything in such a craft and get away scot free. So I was delighted when my neighbor Bill Butman, who happened to have one of those beautiful little double-enders, generously offered it to me. Off I went to bring in my traps.

Soaked as they were, each trap weighed about 60 pounds. When I got them all aboard, with their weight resting on the thwarts and their ends hanging overboard, there was nearly 800 pounds of wood balanced across the gunwales of that little boat.

Picture me headed back on that cold day, rowing like hell to get my load ashore, then add a sudden roll that my skimpy weight couldn't counterbalance, and the traps all sliding overboard. I was too badly scared even to try to pick them up.

Had the traps caught on anything instead of going clean overboard, that error in judgment could have cost me my life. My mistake was to believe that when people said a boat was seaworthy, it was seaworthy, period. True enough, that peapod, properly handled, would get you through a lot of weather, and so would the dory. In either one you could probably survive a considerable gale by lying stretched out right on the bottom to keep your weight down low. But it never occurred to me to test the conditions under which the peapod really was seaworthy.

But ever since that day, I have never designed or built a boat without trying it out before I turned it over to an owner—and I mean giving it the works! Nor have I ever accepted what any designer, builder, or owner says about the seaworthiness of any given boat.

In a rudimentary way, my experience that day taught me something basic about boat design: that design, building, and use are locked together in a firm triangle.

When I was old enough for the Navy, I served my hitch. My ship was an airplane hangar, its deck a concrete floor, and its sea the flattest part of Texas. The most exciting command I ever heard was, "Now hear this. Sweepers, man your brooms. Clean sweepdown, fore and aft."

Me a twenty-year man? No way. I scrapped that dream and took a giant leap from Texas to Metinic Island—a dot on the chart south of Penobscot Bay and five miles out to sea from the fishing village of Spruce Head, Maine.

I spent ten years on Metinic, two years on Little Green Island, and eighteen years in the Spruce Head region—a total of thirty years of fishing from boats, designing boats, and building boats. My past is all right around me in my shop today—an anchor from my old dory, a Ritchie box compass with which I had many violent and always futile arguments, coils of potwarp, toggles, and pot buoys all hung overhead ready to be bent on in case I take a whim to go fishing. And, symbolizing my present occupation, a yellow dory sitting on sawhorses, its varnished oak rails all slicked up for its debut at the New York Boat Show.

No—I have no intention of quitting boat-building as long as I can swing a hammer. Or of giving up using boats, either. My happiest hours are spent in the shop and on the water. Perhaps yours will be, too.

2 "Go Build Your Own Boat!"

Boat-building somehow remains a mystery, even today when so many books have been written about it.

There's nothing mysterious about the source of the mystery, though: the old-time master builders, for the most part, meant to keep their trade secrets just that—secret. And they did a first-rate job of it, too.

That tendency continues. Not long ago an eager novice asked a master boat-builder in Camden, Maine, "How do you determine the waterline?"

"You have to use your head," was all the answer he got.

So, while the oft-heard saying that "you can't take it with you" may apply to material things, it doesn't go for the expert craftsman who most definitely takes his skills with him into the grave.

The motivation is easy to understand, and I don't condemn the old builders for their attitude. In the past, the tricks of the master's trade were passed along to only a select few simply because such secrecy meant survival. Therefore, the average workman who fastened planking all day long was never taught how the planks were lined off for cutting to shape.

For me, a fisherman, there was no protection after I had spent years learning the best fishing bottoms and when to expect lobsters in a certain area: some newcomer would drop his traps right alongside mine. But all the master builder had to do was keep his drawings locked away and his mouth clamped shut. Until relatively recently, there were few if any books on boat-building. The last thing the typical expert craftsman wanted was to have his private expertise sold over the counter.

Today, of course, there are scads of books on building boats in wood, fiberglass, steel, and aluminum. In fact there are so many printed versions of doing the same thing, so many complex approaches to really simple problems and so many volumes of building plans lacking the necessary step-by-step explanations for translating them into boats that the net result is just as if the master builders were still in control, keeping the true secrets of their craft a mystery.

Take, for example, the modern-day do-it-yourselfer who decides to build a sixteen-foot round-bottom utility outboard, and picks up an architect's plan for something to his liking. Almost immediately he gets lost in the terminology alone, before even getting to the required construction techniques. How does our would-be builder go about turning all those lines into a three-dimensional boat?

Unfortunately, most don't.

But don't let this scenario stop *you*. I've been there; I've pondered the beautiful plans and given up. I've also spent plenty of time around boatyards watching the pros doing it, and learning just enough to convince myself that I couldn't.

But I've also built boats, and if Payson can do it, so can you.

What changed my attitude of "I can't" to "maybe I can" was watching my father-in-law, Archie Rackliff—who I knew had no more boat-building skill than I did—design and build two round-bottom sixteen-footers. One, the *Hawk*, was to be his Sunday pleasure boat; the other, *Spit*, was to be a working lobster boat.

Archie, like me, couldn't read blueprints, so what he designed and built had to come out of his head. His approach might be called "action designing" without the benefit of plans. But he was a skilled house carpenter, had been around boats all his life, and was also blessed with both an excellent sense of humor that allowed him to carry on despite mistakes and the determination to see any project he started right through to the end.

To be brief, in building his lobster boat *Spit* he first shaped a keel from a piece of oak about 2-by-2½ inches in cross-section, curving its bottom edge to the amount of rocker that suited him. He then made the midships mold, based on his judgment that the beam should be about one-third the length of the boat, shaped it to what he considered the cross-section of a good seaboat and made it fast to the keel. He next shaped the transom—narrower than the mid-mold—according to his judgment, and braced it in position at the after end of the keel. After this he made a stem, shaped as he thought it should be, and fastened it at the forward end. When, upon stepping back and looking over the set-up, he came to the conclusion that "there ain't enough molds." He added two more fore and aft, braced everything off to external supports, and began planking with ⅝- by 1-inch square edged pine strips, edge-glued and edge-nailed to each other. Then he sprung in a few light, flexible frames, and with the addition of thwarts and gunwales, *Spit* was finished with little fuss or bother. She served many years in the capacity expected of her.

Archie's second boat, *Hawk*, called for something a little different, since he wanted a hull that could take a brand-new ten-horsepower Mercury Hurricane outboard and get all the speed that could be wrung out of it.

He stuck to the same length and beam, but this time he made the keel perfectly straight to give the boat as long and flat a run as possible. He shaped a transom that was as wide and maybe even slightly wider than the beam at the boat's mid-section, and made transom corners at the waterline square to keep her from squatting and to give her stability in tight turns.

Like *Spit*, *Hawk* was strip-planked, but because Archie knew she was going to be faster and stiffer, he decked her over forward and gave her narrow washboards with a raised coaming all around to keep out the sea.

Hawk, too, was a success; one of the fastest boats in the area at a time—in the early 1950s—when the ten-horsepower Mercury was a big engine.

Watching all this inspired me, and I decided that I, too, would build a boat. In my enthusiasm, I asked my still quite new father-in-law if I could use his molds. Without the slightest hesitation, Archie said, "No," and quickly added, "Go build your own boat."

I was shocked. Ordinarily he was a give-the-shirt-off-his-back kind of guy. Moreover, he had no further use for the molds.

My next reaction was "OK—to hell with you, I *will* build my own boat!" Which, inspired now by anger, I promptly set to work doing.

That anger lasted long enough to carry me right through to the end. I strip-planked my boat, just as Archie had done. It was a good boat, too, and it even looked good—good enough for a first boat, anyway.

It was some time before I came to realize that Archie had done me a favor.

3 Early Catastrophes

After my first successful effort, my goal was to build a typical round-bottom carvel-planked lobster boat. I had soaked up the atmosphere greedily as a kid—the steam-bent frames being sprung into place, the hollowing of the planks, the beveling for the caulking seams, the growing mound of sweet-smelling cedar shavings. I wanted to be part of that.

But while feeling quite cocky about the success of my "by-guess-and-by-God" boat, I had sense enough to realize I wasn't ready to undertake such a hull, and instead went on to build two more strip-planked boats while gathering courage to tackle the more sophisticated carvel-planking technique. It was with the first of these that I had my first two disasters—or, looking on the bright side, lessons.

I had somewhere picked up a set of plans for a round-bottom boat called the *Dolly Varden*. They were drawn in terms of half-inch lifts, as though taken from a model built up of horizontal half-inch boards, so that each division of the hull was parallel to the waterline. The plans called for strip-planking, with the added refinement that each strip was hollowed on one edge and rounded on the other. This boat would be about a foot narrower than my first one.

Disaster one got its start when I succeeded in finding what seemed to me to be a pile of perfect boat lumber: nice, wide, straight-grained and clear pine boards, all over sixteen feet long. They had been stacked overhead and under cover for years, and were dry as a bone. The old man who owned the wood thought so, too, and hated to part with it. But persistence won the day and I struck out for home with my treasure.

Worrying that the old man might suddenly change his mind, I immediately cut the pine into strips upon getting home. The new cutters in my molding head and a jig to hold each strip against the ripsaw guide without chattering made short work of it, and I soon had a pile of strips good for nothing but building a boat.

It was easy to make the molds. The boat was drawn on a scale of one inch equals one foot, so that each half-inch lift represented six inches, easily seen as waterlines—as all horizontal lines parallel to the actual waterline are called—on the stem-to-stern profile drawing. The same was true for the body lines from port to starboard. The hollowed and rounded edges of the strips made them self-adjusting, so I didn't even have to bevel them.

She was soon ready to launch, but first I displayed her at a local boat show. The boat got a lot of admirers but no takers, so I hauled her home and left her on the trailer with a tarpaulin over her.

Soon after this, it rained for a couple of days, and when I raised the tarp to see if the boat had taken on any water, I was shocked. I had framed her rail to rail and carefully snugged the frames down against the planking. But now there was a three-quarter-inch gap between the frames and the planking right at the turn of the bilge, starting with the aftermost frames and decreasing progressively forward as the bilge slackened.

In the first place, the planking had been too dry. As it absorbed moisture from rain-damp air, it had swelled, causing the hull to grow in girth. In the second place, the frames had refused to stretch to accommodate the planking (wood doesn't swell very much lengthwise). So with two opposing forces battling each other, something had to give. In this case, the screws holding the planking to the frames had pulled out at the turn of the bilge.

That I had framed the hull with each frame consisting of a single piece of wood going from one rail, down across the keel, and up to the other rail provided the finishing touch. In effect you might say I had hooped a tightly-fitted barrel from the inside. This type of framing is okay with a lapstrake hull, because the overlapping planks can slide by each other with no strain on the frames, but not with rigid planking, edge snug against edge, either strip or carvel.

The dismaying aspect of this disaster was that for months I had had the solution right under me every day while I was hauling my traps. I was using a nice little fourteen-foot carvel-planked wherry I had bought from Alton Whitmore, a Rockport, Maine, builder who, though then in his seventies, still had the eyes and hands for building a good boat. I had used that wherry lobster fishing off Metinic in all kinds of weather, and she had proved to be an excellent boat—very flat on the bottom, with a gentle rocker, easily rowed or driven with a five-horsepower motor, and steady as a rock.

The key to my problem lay in Alton Whitmore's frames, each of which was two timbers with each half coming down from the rail to butt over the keel. The floor timbers set halfway between the frames crossed over the keel. I had never given any thought to the reason for this construction. But with my recent disaster to show me, now I knew, and when I finally began building carvel-planked boats, Alton's way became my way, too.

I still see some boats framed rail to rail. Just before I quit lobstering, a fellow fisherman was complaining to me that his boat leaked. A quick look into his boat's bilges showed the same sorry condition I had managed to achieve: rail-to-rail framing, which caused the fastenings to pull out and the frames to lift off the planking, and building up so much stress that some of the frames had cracked at the turn of the bilge.

It seemed a shame because the boat was an excellent model, and the planking was good as new. Worse yet was that her owner's solution had been to cram more and more wads of cotton into the widened seams to stop the leaking, which only compounded the problem by adding still more stress to the overburdened structure of the hull. This boat finally became unusable and had to be abandoned.

If it had been framed correctly to start with, its hull undoubtedly would have lasted as long as its owner wanted to go on fishing.

My second disaster was simply my attempt to sell my ill-fated second strip-planked boat. Can you imagine trying to convince a prospect to shell out hard cash for a boat that you're feverishly bailing out to keep her from sinking while he stands on the pier watching you demonstrate it?

Obviously, I had to replace the whole mess before I could find a buyer.

4 Feeling Your Way

One reason I call this chapter "Feeling Your Way" is that by experience with other boats I "felt" my way toward the boat I wanted. The second reason is that with a model, your sense of touch as well as sight comes into its own. You can see your boat with your fingertips and your eyes at the same time. In a sense you have your whole boat in your hands—something that is not possible with the full-scale version.

The graduate work in my particular school of naval architecture was done in the same classroom as my undergraduate work—the five-mile run from Spruce Head to the north end of Metinic Island, which took from thirty to forty-five minutes depending on the weather and how hard you wanted to push your boat. Over a ten-year period, the round trips plus the hours on the grounds added up to a lot of running time.

I usually left my fourteen-foot wherry at the island and ran back and forth to "the Main," as many old boatmen used to call the mainland, either with my brother-in-law Edgar Post or with Walter Post (no relation). Both had thirty-foot powerboats built in Friendship; they were of the semi-skeg type, with fine lines and almost wedge-shaped hulls, having a considerable deadrise—the slope from the keel up to the turn of the bilge—and a deep forefoot. They were easy hulls to plank up, but far from comfortable for working. Their constant rolling would wear you down after a while, even in calm weather. Surprisingly, though, their rolling never got much worse in rough weather, and with a moderate head swell they provided a fairly soft and gentle ride. In fact, their underwater shape wasn't too different from that of a Friendship Sloop, which was probably in their ancestry. But under power instead of sail, they didn't have the steadiness and easy motion of a Friendship. If you think of them as dismasted sailboats, you'll have a notion of their behavior in a sea.

They were good sea boats, for while you had to watch your steering with a sea on your stern quarter, you probably couldn't have flipped them. Edgar Post claimed he had tried when his was fresh from the builder, and even with the boat unloaded hadn't been able to do so. Personally, I had no urge to find out for myself.

On the morning after a very cold night, with heavy frost on everything, there would be anywhere from two to half a dozen boats all striking out at once. About halfway to Metinic, the wind would loom up as a long dark line on the horizon. But being in company, no one wanted to be the first to turn back, so we all kept going whether it made sense or not. In the fall I used to double up with Edgar, both of us fishing from his boat, and we would stick it out until we could no longer see the pot buoys in the building seas. Then we would head home, with the worst to come.

If the wind was southwest, our north-by-east-a-half-east course to Spruce Head put the ten- to twelve-foot seas right on the port quarter, each one doing its damnedest to twist us around and drive our bow toward the bottom. Everything that could move had to be lashed down.

Edgar saw such occasions as good opportunities for a little surfing. He would look back until he saw a building sea that seemed just right. When the sea lifted the stern, he'd give the boat full throttle and swing the bow off for a downhill ride. You could really cover ground that way, and safely, too, as long as you minded your steering. Sometimes you even went over one sea and into another. The bow would bury to the chocks, and we would begin to wonder if she might go over.

One day when I was steering, the bow dug in and kept on digging, and I just couldn't make her bear away. We ended up in the trough, just about dead in the water. As the seas rolled her right down, broke over her, and dumped plenty of water aboard, I thought, "Boy, this is it." But she just let herself be pushed sideways, recovered, and we were in charge again.

Another time, in Walter Post's boat, the wind on our homeward course was northwest and counter to the tide, and we were taking a devil's cauldron on the port bow. The boat was quartering a very steep sea, and suddenly all I saw to starboard was a hole to fall into instead of water. She made a crash landing on her starboard side, and I was still wondering if any planks had been started when a rosy glow up forward told us she was on fire. The door to our anchored-down stove had broken open, and dumped its live coals right on the oily deck. In seconds we were battling flames.

We made it, but experiences like that sharpened my preference for a boat with more bearing forward, one that was not likely to dig in or be dumped onto her beam ends. I knew full well, however, that such a design would not produce the perfect boat. When you gain a little here, you always lose a little there.

Two famous hurricanes, Edna and Carol—both of which struck about two weeks apart in September of 1954—gave my plans a push by reducing my ample supply of traps to splinters. I decided I wanted to both build boats and fish for lobster, which meant that I would have to live on the mainland. It also meant I would need a bigger boat so that I could fish more traps and cover more distance in a shorter time. She would be a round-bottom boat, carvel-planked and built to my own design.

At that time I had a general distrust of boat designers. I wasn't totally critical of their product; I just thought that some knew less about building than I did. And since I felt that designing and building ought to go hand in hand, I believed that if they had the nerve to design boats without knowing any more about building them than some of them obviously did, I could design boats, too.

Why should anyone be timid about striking out on his own? Take a look around almost any sizeable harbor and you'll see ugly boats and pretty boats of all shapes and sizes—most of which seem to work to at least some degree. I'm still convinced that marine architecture is far from an exact science: the sea sees to that.

Since I had already built the *Dolly Varden*—with the reverses and the lessons described in the previous chapter—whose plans had been drawn by Weston Farmer based on a half-model made with lifts, I set about making my own half-model.

Ships have been built from half-models for centuries, and today many well-known designers make models before they submit their finely drawn lines to public view. For instance, even though millions of dollars go into every 12 Meter design destined for the America's Cup competition, a model of each design is always built before any keel is laid. True, these models are used in tank tests to analyze the flow of water around the hull in various attitudes and sea conditions, and such facilities as the Massachusetts Institute of Technology's testing tank are not available to the individual private builder. But you can bet that the 12 Meter designers give them a visual once-over that would shame the most dedicated girl-watcher, taking off a little here and adding a little there long before any miniature hull goes into the tank.

Never mind that we're discussing a half-model rather than a whole one. The second half matches the first. Of course you can if you wish build a whole model, and it can certainly give you pleasure. But for building a boat the only way to make sure that the full-size hull is absolutely identical on both sides, to a gnat's eyelash, is to work from a half model, even if it means sawing your whole model lengthwise down the centerline. Furthermore, you can use a half-model to design any type of boat, whether for oars, sail, or power.

A substantial fringe benefit to building from a half-model is that you will always have the model, either to build from again or to mount on a plaque to decorate your office, living room, or den. It's great for daydreaming, for while your boat may be wintering under a tarp or in a boatyard shed, your idea of her is right there on the wall.

7

5 Down the Scale

I had just watched my father-in-law, Archie Rackliff, streak across in his *Hawk* from Whitehead Island to visit me on Metinic, pushed along by his ten-horsepower Mercury outboard, and was thinking how fast that underrated little mill could drive my fourteen-foot wherry.

"Sure," he said when I asked to borrow his motor, "but she won't go."

And she didn't. When I took off my little Sea-Bee outboard, hung the larger Merc on my transom, and opened her up full bore, I found I was dragging half the water in the Gulf of Maine along behind me.

"The trouble is," Archie said, "that she's narrower on the stern than she is amidships. And because your bottom is cocked up at the stern, the bow reaches for the moon while your stern settles down and takes the whole ocean in tow.

"You've got to think *flat and straight*," he went on. "Don't let your bottom draw in one bit from amidships to the transom, and don't have any rocker in her keel. The more your boat is like a flatiron or a slice of pie, the faster she'll go."

These fundamentals were my guiding light when I designed my new lobster boat. To them I added bits and pieces of knowledge picked up by trial and error, and observations of what seemed to work in the waters in which I planned to use the boat. I also asked other boat owners and builders one hell of a lot of questions.

Designing tools? Well, the most sophisticated one I used was an architect's scale. You do need that, to read off your measurements easily and accurately.

I settled on the one-inch-equals-one-foot scale—a good choice for the novice designer, since it provides a fair amount of accuracy and is easy to adapt to because you need only remember that a half-inch equals six inches, a quarter-inch equals three inches, and so on, down to the smallest division on this scale, about a pencil line wide, which will equal a quarter inch on your full-size plan.

Let's say you've decided your boat will be sixteen feet long with a five-foot beam, and that the stem will rise three feet above the keel and the top of the transom will rise two feet. For your half-model you will need six half-inch lifts to make up the height to the top of the stem. Because half of your five-foot beam translates to two and a half inches on your scale—and you'll want a little leeway when you're roughing the model out to approximate dimensions before beginning your fine shaping—your lift boards should be about three inches wide.

The function of the lifts is to permit the builder to establish the height and width of each mold station in steps from the bottom, or baseline, up to the sheer. Remember that each lift is a horizontal lengthwise slice of the hull, and once the half-model has been shaped each separate lift can be used to measure width from the centerline to the outside curve of hull at a point corresponding to the height of the lift from the baseline. This gives the designer a series of points from which he can generate the curve required for the mold—a cross-section that will determine the shape of the hull from keel to sheer at each station.

To facilitate making these measurements, the lifts can be fastened together with dowels or removable screws, so that each one can be handled separately.

However, I chose an alternative method. I glued my lifts in place permanently, and took the outside curve off the mold stations by bending a strip of lead from baseline to sheer, and then traced around the lead to draw each curve. My reason for doing it this way was to preserve the appearance of the model. With age, lifts that are pegged together eventually begin to look like the loose pages of an old book.

Whichever method you choose, I assure you that designing your boat from lifts is a big step ahead of the by-guess-and-by-God or eyeball method, and definitely opens the door to a fuller understanding of boat design.

If you are cutting the lifts from a single length of wood, make it a few inches longer than the ninety-six inches that 6 times 16 calls for, so that the wood cut away by your saw cuts won't leave you holding one slightly short piece. If you don't have a power thickness planer, take your stick to the local mill and have it taken down to exactly one half-inch. There is a good chance that the mill man will simply wind his machine down until the indicator says one half-inch. Before he runs your stick through, insist on trying a few scraps first, measuring the results to make sure what when your wood comes out of the planer it will be as close to exactly one half-inch as possible.

When you've cut your six sixteen-inch lengths, stack them up sandwich style and make sure they add up to the three inches you'll need for the height of the stem. There is no reason why they shouldn't if they've been planed accurately, but it is still comforting to check everything as you go along.

Now fasten them together, gluing them, if you follow my method, and holding them with a couple of clamps. Don't tighten the clamps until you have laid your stack of lifts, edges down, on a dead-flat surface and made sure that every layer is flush against that surface. You must be fussy here, because one side of that stack of lifts will represent the plane of the centerline of your boat, and it must be flat.

Boats, like houses, have got to start off plumb and square. In a house this begins with the foundation; one little mistake here and the carpenter will find that the rooftree has a boat-builder's sheer. I've seen plenty of houses, especially older ones, that were put together with the "that looks pretty good, nail it" philosophy. The rooms wind up being off square and equipment won't fit where it should.

In boat-building, the point of reference for all measurements is called the baseline—a straight line running the length of the hull. Once struck on the architect's plan or the builder's half-model, the baseline's location never changes. Seen from the end, and extended as a vertical plane, the baseline becomes the centerline from which all width measurements are taken. The inboard side of your half-model is that plane. In profile, the baseline is the line from which all height measurements are taken.

With a straight-keel boat such as the one we're talking about here, you can call the bottom of the boat the baseline. Therefore, using half-inch lifts and a scale of one inch equals one foot, each lift will add another six inches to the height above the baseline, both in profile and when viewed from the ends.

When the glue holding the lifts together is dry, you can start carving your model according to the vision of the boat you carry in your mind's eye.

Begin by determining which end of the block will be the bow and which the stern. Have you ever noticed that when people make a rough sketch of a boat, some always see the boat going from left to right while others see it going from right to left? Make your choice depending on how you, personally, envision the boat.

At the stern end, measure up two feet (two inches) on your scale and mark that point. The stern must be raked at least thirteen degrees if you intend to hang an outboard on the boat, and a little more if you want to be able to adjust motor tilt for varying load conditions. You can determine the angle of rake with a protractor set along your baseline.

Next, draw the stem outline exactly the way you think it should look. Then draw the sheer—the curve that runs from the top of the stem to the top of the transom—with a flexible wooden batten, which you have sawed about one quarter-inch wide and one eighth-inch thick. Bend the batten on the flat, not the edge, adjusting it until it follows what you think is the right curvature and setting it against small tacks driven along the sheer line on the model. The batten guarantees that you will get a fair curve, free of humps or jogs. Now draw in the sheer line along the batten with a pencil, and repeat the process on the opposite side of your block of lifts.

Next, locate your mold stations. For a sixteen-foot boat, five molds will be adequate. You need not be fussy about their placement on a hull of this type, where the bends in the planking won't be that hard. By rule of thumb, start by placing the number 1 forward mold three feet (three inches on your scale) aft of the stem, and space the other four molds two and a half feet apart, with the number 2 mold this same distance aft of number 1. This will leave three feet from the number 5 mold to the transom.

Lay off the mold stations in profile on your model, using a combination square, again on both sides. Then square off each station across the top of the hull. Use station number 3 for the greatest beam—in this case, two and a half feet. Mark the width you want at the stern. And if you want a fast boat, don't make this more

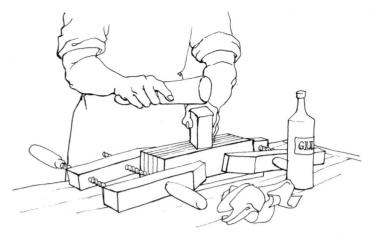

Gluing and setting the lifts.

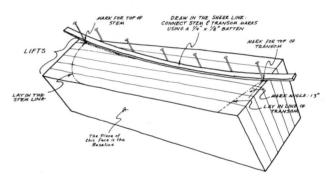

Laying in the profile.

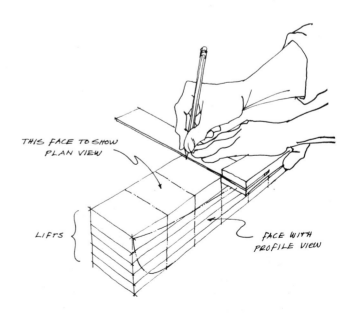

Squaring across the lifts.

than a hair less than the midships section.

Now, working from midships forward, pick the shape you want in terms of the fullness of the bow at the sheerline. Again, use a batten to make this curve on your model. Keep in mind that the more fullness you put into the bow, the more difficult the boat will be to plank up. However, if you want to have some concavity in the forward sides of the hull, you'll have to make the bow section a little more full. There is nothing critical about this shape, except that a little flare forward will help reduce the amount of spray you'll take aboard. The shape above the waterline is mostly for the sake of appearance, though straight sides are better for a work boat, and for steadiness. What is most important is the shape below the waterline—the shape that you'll be riding on.

Now it's time to begin cutting your block to shape. I'm assuming you have a bandsaw or have access to one. Lay the model on its side on the table, which must be set at absolute zero if you're going to get a true right-angle cut. If your blade is a little dull, it will tend to wander, so for peace of mind, allow a healthy one-eighth inch margin and perhaps a little more outside the sheerline as drawn, and make your first cut.

Take the wood you have cut away and tack it right back in place on your block (it has your station lines marked across it).

If you have no bandsaw, use a bowsaw or coping saw for this cut. Lacking both those tools, make a series of handsaw cuts across the top of the half-model down toward the sheerline, but keep the depth of these cuts a little above the line itself. Then chisel away the wood between the cuts and finish the surface down to the sheer with a block plane, spokeshave, and sandpaper.

Returning to the bandsaw procedure, now set the model flat on its bottom and cut around the outside (top view) shape of the hull from stem to stern, again giving yourself an eighth-inch or more leeway. If you have no suitable saws, use a drawknife to remove excess wood from the model's sides, but stop well short of where your serious shaping begins.

Next, with the boat again on its side (and you'll see that it is beginning to look like a boat), saw out the shape of the stem and the raked transom line at the stern. With this, you'll have taken all the big chunks off your block, and the hull will be rough-shaped.

At this point, your next major step is to reduce the top of the model to the sheerline, very carefully smoothing the surface of your sawcut with a small block plane, a spokeshave, and sandpaper. Be especially careful not to round off the edges when the sandpaper runs over them. Remember that on the one-inch-to-one-foot scale you're using, one misguided swipe of the spokeshave or a little heavy-handedness with the sandpaper can in effect cut a half-inch or so off your final product, the full-size boat.

As you work the sheer down, keep checking with your combination square for dead flatness athwartships. You are finished when you've reached the sheerline and no daylight shows under the tongue of the square as you slide it back and forth along the top of the model.

You must now square the station marks across the model's top, and then lay off the outside hull curve along the sheerline. Your last step is to start shaping the bottom, the turn of the bilge and the forward sections. For this a block plane and a spokeshave will take off wood fast enough. Be careful—there's the danger of taking sizeable chunks out of your boat before you've finished building.

It's fascinating to watch the concept of your boat taking shape with every move you make. The more you progress the more exciting the project becomes, until you hate to put it aside.

At this critical stage, however, remember that excitement and eagerness to finish what you've brought along so successfully isn't going to improve your model. If anything, you're likely to improve it out of existence with a too-enthusiastic swish of the spokeshave. Don't do it. Lay your model down and put some distance between it and you. Go for a walk, read a book, go for a sail, chop wood—do whatever you usually do to relax, except getting plastered. Don't go back to the model until you're completely calm.

Now it is sandpaper time. Begin with fairly coarse paper, 60 grit or thereabouts, and get rid of the obvious high spots and tool marks. Again, go easy on the corners and edges—you don't want to round them off. Then proceed with 80 grit paper, and finish off with 100 grit or even finer.

All through this final sanding process, keep studying your model from every angle and stroke it with your fingertips and hands. Touch can detect irregularities your eyes can hardly see. What you are seeking is a model that is as fair as humanly possible, since you are going to take measurements from it. And the model you hold in your hands when finally you say, *"This is it,"* is the boat you'll get when you build from those measurements.

To build the model may take as little as a day, or two or three, and perhaps a few more might turn out a better model. What's your hurry? Model-making is pleasant work and can give much satisfaction.

Satisfied? Okay. Now square each station mark across the outside of the hull from the bottom to the corresponding breadth mark on top of the hull at the sheerline. When you've done this you will have a complete sectional division of your model at each of your five stations.

This was exactly the process I used to make my first model. Nearly every time I made one after that, I did it a little differently and learned a little more. You might want to consider starting out with some of the variations I developed in the process of "feeling my way."

For one thing, you need not make all your lifts the same thickness. There's some virtue in making the top one thicker—say one inch thick instead of a half-inch—because when you saw your sheerline in profile, you won't cut entirely through the top lift and dip into the second one. Instead, you'll get a more pleasing sheerline, unbroken by a slightly shingle-edge effect. You can see how thick to make that top lift so that it will hold the entire curve of your sheerline simply by making a side-view drawing of your lifts all stacked up, and penciling the approximate curve in that you expect the sheer to follow.

On the model of one hull, for decorative purposes I wanted to use a slice of mahogany for the bottom lift. I ended up with a lift of one thickness for the bottom, then a couple more lifts of matching thickness, and a top lift much thicker than any of the others.

You might also consider a variation on the lift technique that I have never used, but which has been widely favored by the designer-builders of large sailing vessels. As I noted earlier, this involves screwing your lifts together instead of gluing them. As the lifts must be absolutely flat against each other, this requires the use of very long screws, placed so that they neither penetrate through the bottom of the model nor lie in the way of any lines you may draw. Also, the screwheads must be countersunk. An alternative is to use shorter screws introduced at varying levels, again with all heads countersunk.

The purpose of this method is to enable the builder to separate the lifts to take the lines off, particularly at the sections, with a little more ease. But we'll go into that in the next chapter.

Of all my models, I have only two left—the one illustrated here and another shaped from a single solid piece of wood. I did that one when I had gained confidence and knew I could scale off the lines without benefit of lifts. However, I recommend that you begin with lifts. This method has obvious advantages and has always been the choice of the professional boatbuilder.

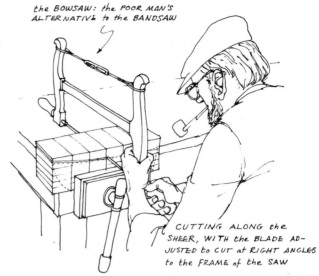

the BOWSAW: the POOR MAN'S ALTERNATIVE to the BANDSAW

CUTTING ALONG the SHEER, WITH the BLADE ADJUSTED to CUT at RIGHT ANGLES to the FRAME of the SAW

Cutting around the outside.

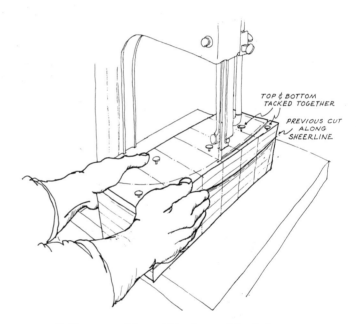

TOP & BOTTOM TACKED TOGETHER

PREVIOUS CUT ALONG SHEERLINE

Cutting around the outside shape of the hull.

Shaping the hull.

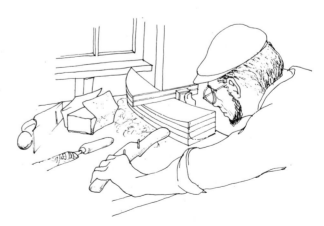

Working the sheer down testing for squareness.

6 Subtracting the Third Dimension

One of the advantages of working from a model is that you get to know your boat in three dimensions from the very beginning. When you reach the point of drawing two-dimensional plans on a sheet of paper, you'll have a better understanding of your goal and how to reach it. A mystery that often sets the first-time builder back on his heels is: How am I ever going to build a nicely curved hull from lines on a flat surface and a bunch of numbers?

With your model, you translated your idea of a boat into a solid, three-dimensional shape. Now you're going to translate that model, with all its graceful curves, into those lines and numbers. And after that, you're going to translate those lines and numbers into a full-size boat. You learn a lot simply by going through these processes. The trick is to make sure you don't leave anything out in the translation.

There are more sophisticated ways of developing the lines of a boat than taking them off a model, the method I first used, but I had no access to them, and it's likely you don't either. Yet the simplest way worked for me, and it will work for you.

To build my boat I needed only two views of her: a profile view, and a view of each of the thwartship sections. The profile provides the curve of the stem and the rabbet line (where your planking fits against the stem and the keel). The view of each section shows the width of each lift at each station, and also the height of each lift at that station, thus providing the wherewithal to produce the cross-section hull curves required for each mold.

I began taking off lines by making two drawings of the lifts just as they were stacked before any wood was taken off. Both drawings were done on the same sheet of paper, one above the other, with their station marks matched up. Then I drew verticals from the bottom drawing to the top drawing at each station, running through both.

Next, I put the half-model, with the flat centerline plane down, on top of the upper drawing, being careful to match up the station lines. I then traced around the model to lay down the profile.

My next step was to take the shape off each section. Beginning at station number 1, I measured its height from the baseline to the sheer on the profile drawing and transferred this height to the same vertical line on the lower drawing. I then measured across the top of the model to get the half-breadth at station number 1, and laid this distance down at right angles to the station line and running aft from the height mark. All that remained to be done then was to find the shape of the cross-section curve of the hull between the outer end of this half-breadth line and the intersection of the vertical station line with the baseline of the hull.

Obviously the easiest way to get this curve would be

to saw right through the model at the number 1 station line and trace the half-breadth section directly from that. No doubt some boatbuilders have done this. But who wants to slice up a beautiful model with hours and hours invested in it?

Instead, I took a thin strip of lead, the type used for chimney flashings, and bent it tightly around the outside of the model at station number 1; I then filed the ends of the strip flush where it met the centerline at the bottom and where it crossed the sheer. When I aligned the strip with these two key points on the bottom drawing I traced around it, and there was the section for that mold.

If this method strikes you as being slightly crude, just remember that for centuries—and not so long ago, either—builders of big ships used it to turn out some very substantial and finely finished hulls. It's quite easy, with a little judicious tamping of a hammer against a piece of wood held tightly against the lead strip, to get a skin-tight fit against the model. More sophisticated methods, used with a little less than practiced skill, might well provide less accurate results.

I repeated this process with stations 2, 3, 4, and 5.

The transom, however, calls for a different approach. Because it is raked, you can't generate its true shape by striking verticals and horizontals. Instead, you simply place the transom of your half-model against the profile drawing and trace around it. The transom is then expanded to full size along the rake of the stern.

I liked having the shapes of the molds drawn right on each station, because I could see exactly what they would look like in cross-section at each station location.

Since I didn't have a table of offsets, which would have given me distances of various points from the baseline up and the centerline out, I put the measurements down right at each station. I also scaled off the widths at each station and entered them on the profile drawing. You can put them anywhere; the point is to know where they are when you need them later.

I didn't draw a third view looking down through the hull from the sheer to the bottom, which would have given me the waterlines—what naval architects call the plan view—because the lifts gave me all I needed to know about the waterlines; the lines between them are waterlines. Nor did I loft from the model, because at that time I didn't even know what lofting was.

Getting out the shape of the stem and the forefoot area was easy. As you can see on the drawing, I simply struck a line from the top of the stem to where the straight keel began, and from that as a base I drew a series of perpendiculars on it, with each one extending to the curve of the stem. Reproduced full-size, the perpendiculars permitted me to reproduce that curve.

Obviously, if you made your lifts detachable, you would be able to manipulate them individually and take

Drawing station marks.

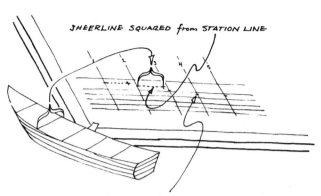

SHEERLINE SQUARED from STATION LINE

HEIGHTS TAKEN OFF in PRECEDING STEP

Half breadth from half model.

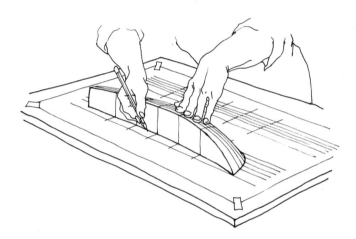

Tracing the profile from the half model.

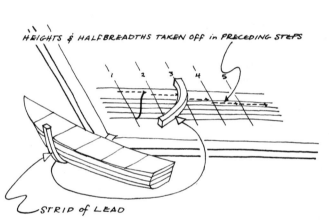

HEIGHTS & HALFBREADTHS TAKEN OFF in PRECEDING STEPS

STRIP of LEAD

Section shape from half model.

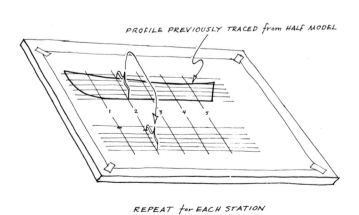

PROFILE PREVIOUSLY TRACED from HALF MODEL

REPEAT for EACH STATION

Section heights from the profile.

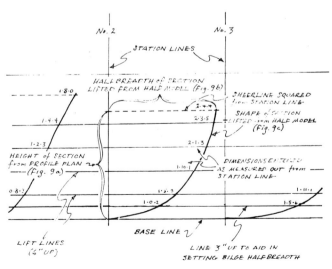

No. 2

No. 3

STATION LINES

HALF BREADTH of SECTION
LIFTED from HALF MODEL (Fig. 9b)

SHEERLINE SQUARED
from STATION LINE

SHAPE of SECTION
LIFTED from HALF MODEL
(Fig. 9c)

HEIGHT of SECTION
from PROFILE PLAN
(Fig. 9a)

DIMENSIONS ENTERED
AS MEASURED OUT from
STATION LINE

BASE LINE

LIFT LINES
(6" UP)

LINE 3" UP TO AID IN
SETTING BILGE HALF BREADTH

Mold dimensions.

measurements from the centerline to both outer edges that would give you intermediate points on the curve of the hull, and you could draw your lines with ease. On the whole, however, I would say making lifts detachable isn't worth the effort, since you can get very accurate sectional curves with the lead-strip technique.

With all the necessary dimensions and shapes now taken off the half-model, I was ready to transfer these elements to full-size patterns on the floor of my workshop, and from these patterns to make the molds, the stem, and the transom, and to set up for building the boat.

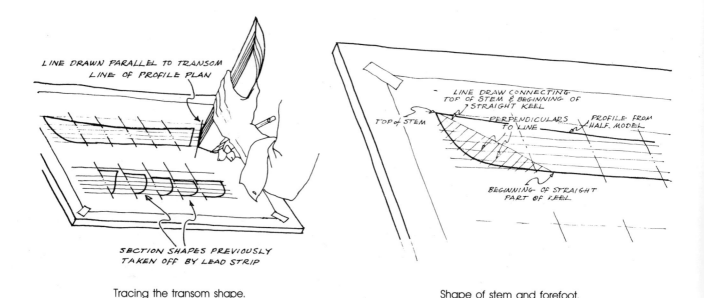

Tracing the transom shape.

Shape of stem and forefoot.

Dimensions of the lobster boat.

7 Setting Up the Backbone

The backbone of your boat's skeleton consists of the keel, the stem, and the transom—the foundation for the frames, the floor timbers, and the planking.

But boat-building wood doesn't fall into your hands for the asking, so step one is to find a source of wood and select the best of it for your purpose, within the limits of your pocketbook. Part of the backbone of your boat, the stem, is curved, so you'll want to find some pieces of wood with a grain that approximates that curve. The keel is straight. Your best source of stock—straight, curved, or crooked—is the pickover pile at the local sawmill.

I'm luckier than most builders because there are several boatyards in my neck of the woods that are large enough to support their own sawmills. At such a yard nearly everything they need for building is sawed out live-edged in flitches—longitudinal slices right out of the trunk of the tree, with the bark still on. From this they choose and saw the best wood for their needs and throw the rest outside in a pile, where you can pick it over until you find what you want to buy. That's where you'll find me.

This doesn't mean I'm looking for second-rate wood; I'm looking for the best. But custom sawing is expensive, and who do you think will get the most attention—the fellow who wants twenty-five dollars worth of oak for a sixteen-footer or somebody who shows up prepared to pay for the boatstock for a hundred-thousand-dollar yacht?

More about grain patterns later; right now you're looking for a straight piece of oak sixteen feet plus in length, out of which you can saw, or have sawed, a piece sided two inches (two inches wide) and two and a half inches deep, for your keel.

That depth is important, because you'll want to have enough keel protruding beyond your hull planking to give a reasonable grip on the water. With five-eighths-inch planking set flush against the top edge of a two-and-a-half-inch spine, this comes to one and seven-eighths inches that will be cutting through the water. I well remember running another fellow's boat down the Spruce Head Island Gut where it curves under a bridge, a tight turn that I ended up sliding around sideways. When I got ashore and checked the keel, I found it was only a little three-quarter nub in cross-section—not adequate for the job it was called upon to perform.

To this keel we are going to fit a stem, also two inches wide, to match it. Lay out the full-size pattern for this stem piece. Begin by measuring the line from the top of the stem to the keel on your drawing, then take it off the drawing with your scale rule and convert it to feet and inches. Draw this line on your shop floor or on a piece of building paper, whichever is most convenient.

Next, measure off the intervals between the squared-off lines that run perpendicular to the outboard profile of the stem on your drawing, again scaling up with your rule, and spot their locations along your scaled-up stem line. Now measure the length of each of these lines and extend them accordingly at the proper intervals on your plan. You're now ready to make a batten to spring to this full-size stem curve.

Laying out the pattern for the stem.

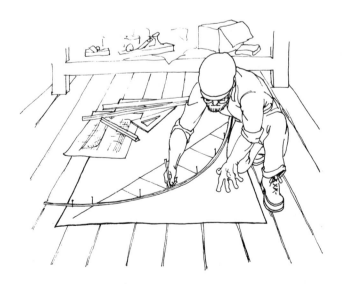

Fairing the stem curve with a batten.

Drive a nail at each end of the straight stem line and also at the end of each of the extended perpendiculars from it where they would intersect the curved stem line. Bend your retractable metal pocket rule around these nails to find the minimum length of batten you'll need, and add another foot so the curve won't go flat at the ends when you bend the batten. Now cut your batten out of quarter-inch square stock. Try springing this around the nails, with each end of the batten extending six inches beyond each of the extreme nails. If the batten is too stiff to follow the curve without signs of breaking, slim it down equally along its entire length until it does bend to a fair curve. Use one-inch-long number 18 wire brads to tack the batten in place, driving them alongside, not through, the batten. Now step back and check the curve for fairness. You've been as accurate as possible with your measurements; now your eyes must take over. If you see a hard or a quick place instead of a smooth curve, recheck your measurements and put a nail here and there until the whole batten does lie in a fair curve. And that's it.

I strongly urge you to make your stem in two pieces—an upper and a lower half—to make it easier to find stock with a grain that follows the stem curve. Intersect the forefoot at the center of the full curve, and lay out the two pieces of wood. And to keep each piece as straight and as narrow as possible, lay out the stem knee where the two pieces join, so that the upper piece sits quite plumb, close to the vertical, and the lower piece lies just about in line with the keel, as though it were an extension of it.

Now figure out how much wood you must leave on the stem face, which is to say the side of its fore-and-aft thickness, after you have cut the rabbet line where the plank ends will notch into each side of the stem, still allowing sufficient wood on the inner side of the stem face, aft of where the plank ends fit into the rabbet. For a boat of this size, three and a half inches at the top of the stem, gradually increasing to about four inches at the stem knee joint and to about four and a half inches where the lower part of the stem joins the keel, will do nicely.

The after part of the stem assembly joins the keel with a lap joint long enough to allow the use of a couple of three-eighths-inch carriage bolts to fasten them together. Two similar bolts can be used to fasten the stem knee to the upper and lower sections of the stem.

To make patterns for these pieces, I use semi-transparent drafting paper and trace directly onto it from my plan on the floor.

At this point I seem to hear voices saying, "But paper swells and shrinks!" and other muttering that paper is so flimsy you will get "edge set," which means bending on the flat, if you use it, which will throw your pattern out of kilter. To take care of both those problems, I tack the paper right down on the area I'm tracing, and before I pick it up I strike a line on it, using either a straight-edge or a chalkline, right across the drawing anywhere there is room. I could roll up that paper and lug it around the world, and when I'm ready to use it all I have to do is check that line against a straight edge. Straight is straight.

We're talking about two pieces of wood for the upper and lower sections of the stem, each with a likely grain for its part of the stem curve. When you've found what you want, most likely near the root cut of one of those flitches sliced right out of a tree where grain tends to sweep up in curves, lay your transparent pattern right down on the stem stock and use an awl to prick small holes right along the curves of the drawing in as many place as you want, then saw the pieces to the prick marks.

There is another way to make the stem assembly, which you may prefer especially if there is no sawmill nearby or you don't have access to wood of suitable size or of an acceptable grain pattern. You can laminate the

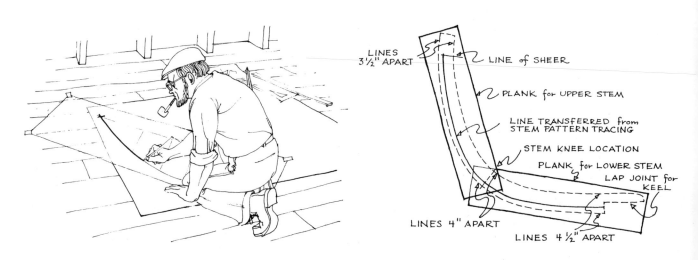

Tracing the pattern for the upper stem.

Stem pattern on planks for cutting.

LINES 3½" APART

LINE of SHEER

PLANK for UPPER STEM

LINE TRANSFERRED from STEM PATTERN TRACING

STEM KNEE LOCATION

PLANK for LOWER STEM

LAP JOINT for KEEL

LINES 4" APART

LINES 4½" APART

stem from relatively thin strips of wood, bending them around the outline you have drawn; this allows you to build up the entire curve of the stem in one smooth bend, all the way to the keel joint.

At this point, some builders get right to work with a chisel and cut the rabbet line, where the forward plank ends fit neatly into this recess in the stem. This is what I do, mainly because I get a good deal of pleasure out of using a good sharp chisel and making this demanding

cut right to a line. Actually, if this prospect scares you, there's no need to cut a rabbet in the stem. Instead, you can plank right to the face of the stem piece, letting the planks run by the stem a little. Then, when you've cut the plank ends off flush with the stem, you can simply cover them both with a stem cap, or false stem, as it's called in my area.

While you're thinking about that, let's get on with the rest of the skeleton.

8 Molds, Transom, and Transom Knee

You may have noticed that in the drawing showing the model, the lifts are all parallel to the baseline. In fact, in making the model, I cut the bottom lift away below the waterline, giving it a slant making it impossible for this lift to be parallel to the others. However, when I designed the model this way I outsmarted myself because it meant that I could no longer set up the boat plumb and square. I either had to slant the keel in order to keep the molds plumb vertically, or set the keel level and cant the molds up to the amount indicated by the half model. Or did I?

This brings out the advantages of working for yourself instead of for a customer. Since I had my building stocks all set up for a level keel, I went right ahead and tilted the molds aft by the required amount. But then, preferring to avoid unnecessary bother, I tried setting them plumb. It made hardly a smidgin of difference in

the hull shape, because this design is essentially a box-section hull.

I cursed my stupidity in not foreseeing this complication, for my rough-and-ready solution didn't get me all the way off this particular hook; with the bottom lift cut on a slant, I had to change my working baseline to the top of the lift, and then get the mold heights by measuring from the sheer down to the baseline and from the bottom of the hull back up to it, adding the two figures.

This is a cautionary tale, whose moral is: Don't do what I did. Stick with parallel lifts as they're described and drawn in Chapter 6—with the bottom of the model right spang on the baseline and the bottom of each mold landing on it also. You will, of course, have to measure the height of the sheer at each station, but this is a simple matter when you work from a hull-bottom baseline.

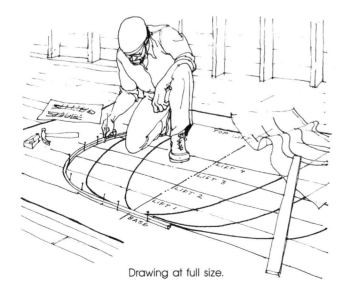

Drawing at full size.

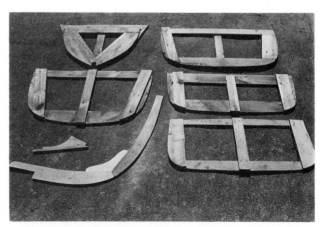

Four stem-assembly molds (above), half a breasthook (lower left), and a transom pattern (lower right).

The mold is drawn at each station from measurements taken off the half-model and stepped up to full size. For each station, you need draw only one curve—half-breadth mold—on your shop floor. You can then lay tracing paper over that, transfer the line to the paper, and reverse the paper to get the other half of the mold (making sure that the centerline and the top of the sheer are right on the money).

If you find that your lift thicknesses don't provide enough reference points to ensure a fair and accurate curve, use your scale rule to strike off intermediate points from your half-model body-section tracing—as many as you need to make you feel confident that you're arriving at a truly accurate full-size station mold. As you did with the stem pieces, use a light batten to connect the points.

Superimposing the mold drawings on your scaled-down plan, working from the same centerline and baseline, will save time and space in translating the molds to full size. It's best to begin with the widest beam, so start by drawing a straight line across the top of the widest half-breadth taken from your model, as indicated on your original scaled-down tracing, and doubling its length to represent the full width of the boat at the top of the widest beam.

At the center of this line, strike off another line that will represent the depth of this mold, or its height above the baseline. This line will also serve as a centerline on your full-size plan. Now draw in your curves for each station, using the same centerline and baseline, and all your full-size section plans will be contained inside the largest mold section in one place on your shop floor.

Obviously, when you plank over these molds whose outside edges represent the inside skeleton of your hull, your boat is going to grow in size by the thickness of the planks. If you want to avoid this slight increase in hull girth, set your dividers to the plank thickness and with the point pivoting on various locations on the mold line, swing a series of arcs inside the curve. Drive brads at strategic bend locations, and spring a batten to get the new inside-of-planking curve for each station.

Marine architects almost invariably draw their plans to the outside of the planking. The reason for this is obscure, at least to me, unless it aids the architect in making closer displacement calculations. The practice may simply have evolved naturally from the earlier, universal custom of working from a half-model. On the other hand, some architects draw their plans to the inside of the planking, so it's advisable to read the notes on any architect's plan you may use to find out which way he has chosen to draw a particular boat.

Molds can be made from pine, spruce, or just about anything else that will hold a nail; molds are not an integral part of the boat's structure. Don't bother with beveling the molds' edges; just saw them out square. But do be sure that you set molds that are forward of amidships *aft* of the station lines, and that you set the molds that are aft of amidships *forward* of the station lines. This will ensure that your planking will bear on the edge of each mold that represents the shape you have designed for your hull at that point.

Now for the transom and the stern knee.

It's highly unlikely that you will find a board wide enough to let you make the transom in one piece. I built mine from two pieces of one-inch oak, grooving the edges of both pieces where they joined and fitting them together with a spline—a strip of soft wood between them that exactly filled the grooves—to make a watertight joint.

You can make these grooves on your table saw by making a single cut to the depth you want, and then progressively adjusting the saw fence outward after each pass until you have gained the desired groove width. To make sure these grooves will be exactly aligned, make your starting cut on each half of the transom, alternating the two pieces for each succeeding cut; this will ensure that you are using the same fence setting on both. As the ripsaw blade you will use for this takes out a bite of an eighth inch or a little less, you'll probably need three passes. If you have a set of dado cutters—a group of small saws linked side by side—you can cut each groove in one pass.

The shape of the transom is transferred from the full-size drawings using the method described previously for the molds.

You will need framing around the inboard edges of your transom to provide the wood for taking nails when you're fastening the planks to avoid having to nail directly into the transom edge grain. Edge-grain nailing, with the nail and the wood grain going in the same direction, makes a weak joint. Alton Whitmore's old

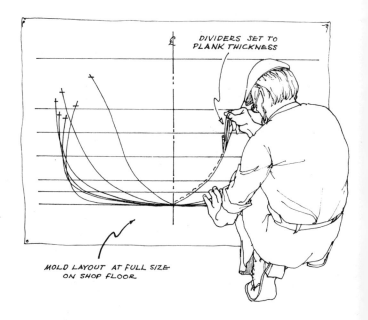

DIVIDERS SET TO PLANK THICKNESS

MOLD LAYOUT AT FULL SIZE ON SHOP FLOOR

Adjusting for plank thickness.

wherry was nailed this way, and the planks have come slightly adrift around the transom.

Before you start cutting the transom framing, note that because the transom is raked aft, its bottom must be beveled. To make an accurate bevel, you need a bevel square and a bevel board. I've never seen the latter for sale anywhere, but every shop should have one, so you'd better make yours right now.

A bevel board is simply a flat piece of wood—about five inches wide and twenty-two inches long will do—with a series of angled lines drawn across it that will allow you to read angles off your bevel square. I recommend three-eighths-inch marine plywood for your board. Set your bevel square at 0 degrees and draw a line across the board about two inches below the top. Below this, draw lines for one degree, two degrees, three degrees, and so on all the way to 45°.

You can do this with a protractor, but reading the angles off the table-saw indicator is more accurate. Crank the table one degree at a time, each time setting the bevel square to fit the angle of the table, and use the tongue of the square to transfer the angle to the board. The degree label and the accompanying line must be carefully inked in for each step. When you've drawn in all forty-six lines—zero through forty-five—drill a hole in the top of the board, run a cord through it, and hang it where it will be handy. You'll be using it a lot.

I should mention that tool makers vary in their adjustment markers. Most of my tools are marked from 0 to 45 degrees, but my table saw reads from 45 to 90 degrees, meaning the same thing. Don't let such variations fool you.

At this point, let's get some of the boat's backbone elements together, beginning with the stem assembly and the keel. Clamp the stem knee to the stem assembly, applying any standard bedding compound such as those produced by the leading paint manufacturers. Next, mark off the locations of the bolts and drill the holes for them, from the outside of the stem in. Bore for the bunghole first, judging its size by the diameter of the carriage-bolt head whose countersink the bung will

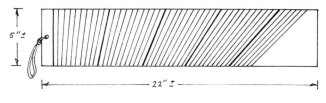

The bevel board.

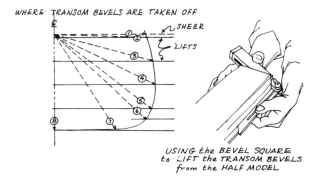

Lifting bevels from the half model.

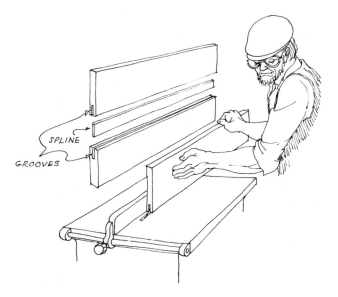

Transom splines.

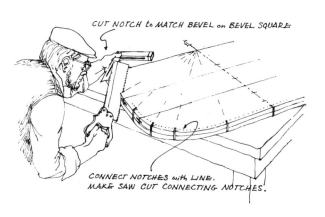

Transferring bevel to transom.

cover, and then bore for the bolt itself. If you bore in reverse order, the bunghole bit will have nothing to center on and will wobble out an egg-shaped hole that no bung will ever plug. If you should forget and bore the bolt hole first, plug it with wood so the bunghole bit will have something to bite into.

The next step is to fasten the stern or transom knee to the keel with two bolts. Again, start by drilling bung holes on the bottom of the keel, through which these bolts will pass before they go through the knee. Then fasten the transom to the knee with two more bolts, drilling the bungholes starting at the after face of the transom. It is important to give these bolts adequate spacing while making sure that no bolt will interfere with another.

Now is a good time to mark off the outside rabbet line as seen in profile on the half-model. The thickness of your hull planking is to be five-eighths inch, and the molded depth of the keel is two and a half inches. Therefore, set your combination square at one and seven-eighths inches—just what you will have left between the bottom of the keel and the bottom of the planking when it is butted against the keel and flush with its top.

Now, using your combination square, start at the top of the face of the stem and scribe a curve that is one and seven-eighths inches from and exactly matching the outside curve of the stem. Carry this curve down along the forefoot and back along the keel. In the section of the hull where the molds have no deadrise, no rabbet need be cut, because the inside edge of the garboard—the plank next to the keel—will lie flat against the face of the keel. The rabbet will be cut where it is needed to provide square-edge fit for the garboard forward, where the plank has an upward twist. You now know exactly where the outside of the rabbet will fall. Don't cut it yet.

Now to set up the backbone. How far off the floor of your shop should it be, and on what shall it sit? When I do this I cut enough two-by-fours eighteen inches long

to support the length of the boat when they are spaced out and in a row and set upright. I then notch the tops of these short lengths to accept the width of the keel, tie them all together with a couple of boards, and nail cross-pieces to their bottoms to keep them upright.

The eighteen-inch height allows enough distance between the bottom of the boat and the shop floor to let you drive in fastenings while planking the bottom. A mechanic's dolly will allow you to roll from one end of the hull to the other while you're doing this, until you reach the turn of the bilge; you won't need the dolly after that. The entire assembly is mounted on a longitudinal strongback that is fastened to the shop floor. However, before you nail that strongback down, make sure to place it where you can walk around the hull comfortably, with plenty of room to work with reasonable freedom.

Next set the keel in place in the notches provided. Make sure the stem is plumb, and fasten the top of it to the wall or to a beam overhead, with a long stick or brace nailed to a stud or a rafter—any way that you can devise to make it really secure from wobble. Brace off the transom similarly, and begin erecting the molds on their proper stations along the keel. Nail them in place, for these are temporary installations and will be removed when the hull is completed.

The first mold must be notched the full two inches of keel thickness, because it will sit on the after part of the stem assembly where the assembly joins the keel. The other molds will sit on top of the keel, matched centerline for centerline at each station.

Again, fasten each mold overhead to some member in the ceiling, making sure that each mold is plumb fore and aft and square to the keel. In my shop, I nailed a board across the rafters in line with the set-up, directly over the keel, and fastened the molds to that, using any sticks sufficiently strong to brace them off securely.

Your skeleton set-up is already beginning to look like a boat, and with the longitudinal ribbands in place she'll look even more so.

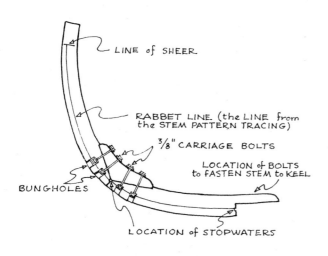

The stem assembly.

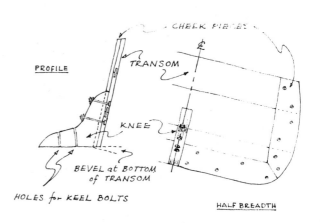

Transom and knee assembled.

Building the strongback.

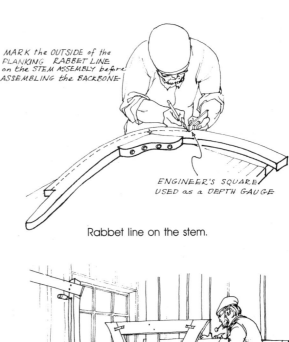

MARK the OUTSIDE of the
FLANKING RABBET LINE
on the STEM ASSEMBLY before
ASSEMBLING the BACKBONE

ENGINEER'S SQUARE
USED as a DEPTH GAUGE

Rabbet line on the stem.

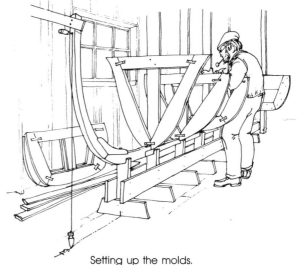

Setting up the molds.

9 Ribbands, Rabbets, and Frames

Ribbands are temporary "strakes" that run the length of a boat hull. Fastened at intervals to the stem, the molds, and the transom, they form a basket into which you can bend the frames. They must therefore be strong enough to stand the stress of the bending process. After all the frames are in and you begin to plank, you'll remove the ribbands one by one as each successive port and starboard pair of planks replaces them.

Saw out your ribbands from pine, fir, or whatever wood you fancy, making them about one-inch square, or the thickest square cross-section you can bend without breaking.

Eighteen or twenty ribbands—nine or ten to each side—will do for a hull of this size. You shouldn't have any trouble finding pieces of wood that are long enough, but if you do, butt two short lengths together and fasten a piece of the same size stock over the butt joint.

Your sheerline heights have to be marked on the molds, the stem, and the transom; a pencil mark will do. Now wrap one of your ribbands around one side and see how it looks. Since you haven't yet cut a rabbet into the stem, take a chisel and cut it in now, using this sheer ribband as a bevel guide. Chisel the rabbet five-eighths of an inch deep where the ribband falls on the stem, and where the hood ends of the planking will lie. Don't cut any deeper.

You need not be fussy when you spring on the ribbands. Merely space them out by eye in such a way that they will be able to take the pressure of the frames when you bend them in. Now measure the girth of your hull from the keel to the sheer at the transom, amidships, and at the bow, and start the first ribband a few inches out from the keel on each side. Keep adding the ribbands, moving up the sides, cutting a notch at the stem rabbet line for each one. Always match the ribbands port and starboard; don't install ribbands on one side ahead of the other or they'll exert a twisting force that will result in a misshapen hull.

With the ribbands on, you've reached a real morale-building stage of your construction. You can now see, by following the lines of the ribbands, how the hull planking will look.

However, before the frames go in, the entire rabbet has to be cut on both sides—one of the trickiest parts of boat-building. The first time I did this I asked one of the old-time builders I knew just how the garboard plank (the first plank next to the keel on each side—also known as the garboard strake) sits in its rabbet.

"Do you take any wood off the inside of the plank to make it fit?" I asked.

"No," he said. "The garboard sits in the rabbet square-edged, and the hood ends, the forward ends of the planking that fit into the stem, sit in square-edged too."

He also pointed out that when the garboard rabbets have been cut and the forward frames are going in, they too are boxed into the keel in a recess that accepts the full thickness of the frame, and are never shaved or tapered to shortcut the process of chiseling out that recess. You need the strength this provides, because each plank that you twist into place and fasten to a frame will try to twist off and straighten out again, attempting to pull the frame with it. (Like all my question-and-answer sessions with such men, I made this one very brief, to get the essentials without wearing out my welcome.)

It's easy to determine the rabbet bevels you'll need right at each station: the rise of the molds at these points will show you exactly how much of a bevel, or slant, you must establish in the bottom of the rabbet to give the plank a square-edged fit. The spaces between the molds are what you'll wonder about, especially in the area from just aft of the first mold on up to the stem, a distance of about four feet on this hull. The

garboard plank stays almost flat from the transom to this stretch and then gradually twists as it runs forward until it is almost plumb where its hood end lands in the stem rabbet.

I based my solution on a light batten, one-eighth inch thick and three-quarters of an inch wide and about four feet long. On one of its ends I nailed a piece of wood of plank thickness and on the other end a piece of my framing timber, with the batten set flush by inlaying it in both pieces to a depth equal to its own thickness. All I had to do was bend that batten to fit close against the inside of the battens and then, using the outside rabbet line already drawn on the keel as a guide, place my piece of planking material against the keel, just as the garboard plank itself would lie. Where the top edge of my planking sample struck the keel was where the top rabbet line would fall, and where I would make my cut; and by observing the angle at which the square edge of my piece of planking met the keel I could determine the angle of the interior bevel required to make a square-edged fit between the edge of the garboard and the bottom surface of the rabbet.

It's wise to get the rabbet off to a smooth start on the after part of the keel so that shallow rabbet cuts will flow gently and gradually into the deeper cuts forward near the bow. In the stern area, where the garboard meets the keel square on, no cuts and consequently no bevels are needed. At about the midships point, the planking sample began striking the face of the keel at a slight angle, showing that a shallow rabbet cut would have to be made to permit the edge of the garboard to make a square-edged contact with the wood of the keel, and I marked where the top edge of my piece of portable planking touched the keel. Moving along forward I spotted a series of such marks; then, using a long flexible batten to make a fair curve, I connected all the spots to draw the upper line of the rabbet for my chisel and plane to follow.

In the keel near the forefoot area, I slid the batten down across the ribbands, intersecting them just about the way the molds did, but on the stem, which was rising toward the vertical, I ran my feeler batten along

Hull—ribboned and framed, with rabbet line cut, and with garboard and #1 plank on. (Photo by Alden Philbrook)

Bending on the ribbands.

with the flow of the ribbands to make my marks.

Then I was ready to start cutting the rabbet into the keel and stem. To make the job easier, I used a five-eighths-inch chisel—the same width as the plank thickness—to cut the depth, and I used a wider chisel to fair the line lengthwise. A rabbet plane is fine where the going is straight, but in curved areas you must use a sharp chisel, and a scraping motion, to cut out the rabbet cleanly.

All through the cutting process I kept my feeler batten right at hand, bending it down tight to the ribbands as before and shoving its piece of planking stock right against the rabbet, repeating the process until it told me that the cut was deep enough and had the right bevel—a good wood-to-wood contact.

When you're satisfied that your garboard plank will lie in its rabbet in a nice fair line, lay off the frame locations on the keel. I used one-inch-by-three-quarter-inch oak for my frames, and placed them on eight-inch centers—that is, spaced eight inches from the center of one frame to the center of the next. Aft of the keel-joint/stem assembly, running to the stern, fitting the frames is no problem, because the ends of the matching port and starboard frames are simply butted together at the centerline of the keel, and each one is nailed down to the top of the keel (I'll pursue the matter of fastenings when we get to the point of actually putting in the frames).

Again, the twisty part of the hull forward is where complications arise. There the frames are recessed into the deadwood part of the stem assembly that sits on top of the stem-to-keel joint. The aftermost frames in this are boxed into the deadwood at about the same angle as that shown for the mold at station number 2, with each set of frames increasing the angle as they near the bow.

Now it's time to use the other end of my feeler batten, the end with a piece of framing stock fastened to it.

You use it exactly the same way you used the planking stock end to mark for your garboard rabbet, only this time you are placing the end of the piece of framing stock against the rabbet itself, for the frames are recessed into the face of the rabbet, and the planking was recessed into the face of the keel before the rabbet was cut.

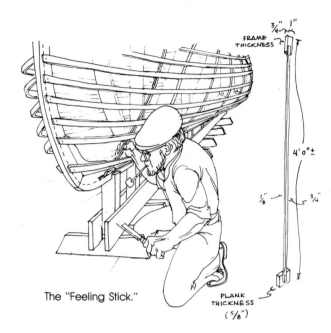

The "Feeling Stick."

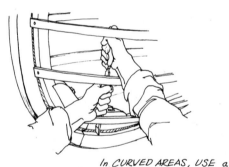

In CURVED AREAS, USE a
CHISEL with a SCRAPING MOTION

Cutting the rabbet.

The GARBOARD SITS
in the RABBET
SQUARE EDGED

Box for frame

GARBOARD
STRAKE

Sec. AA

PLANK

The HOOD ENDS of the
PLANK SIT SQUARE EDGED
in the STEM RABBET

Sec. BB

Stem Assembly
Sections

Garboard and hood ends.

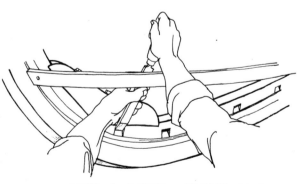

AFTER the RABBET is FINISHED, BOXES
for the FRAMES are CUT inside the RABBET

Boxing for frame timbers.

Because you quite literally feel your way along using this method, "batten feeler" or "feeling stick" seems like an appropriate name for this device. I've never seen anyone else use it, or even mention it, but I am willing to bet that there are other users.

One advantage of using the feeling stick when you're working with the forward frames is that its batten lies against the ribbands in the same way that your frames will lie when they are being steam-bent into place. The stick gets the job done precisely, and in a very simple way. It's likely that if I had taken the trouble to read every book that deals with the twisty bevel-cutting problem, I'd have been so confused I might very well have never started. I've read many complex approaches to boat-building problems that really have simple solutions. I say do it the easy way and get smart later.

With the rabbets cut port and starboard, the frame locations laid off, and box cuts made in the rabbets to receive them, we can now bend in the frames.

White oak seems to be the recommended favorite for frame stock, and I suppose that's the reason it's hard to come by. I've never used white oak. I use what's available, and where I live red oak is it.

Red oak has been accused of being short-lived, but it's good for twenty to thirty years and longer in salt water; it also takes steaming or boiling well, and is the choice of boat-builders all along the Maine coast. However, this is not so in fresh water. I've seen an open—and therefore well-ventilated—lobster-boat-style craft used on the Belgrade Lakes here in Maine, whose red oak quickly went so soft you could pick pieces of frame out with your fingers. I recommend that you use the wood that has proved itself in boats in your own locality.

Whatever stock you choose, picking the best of it for bending is very controversial. I've read one self-proclaimed expert who insisted, in print, that the best wood to use was that cut from a tree that had stood alone and was therefore used to bending with the wind. I can't disprove that, but I will say that I've never been tempted to ask a mill operator the life stories of the trees from which he cut his lumber. Too shy, perhaps. So I just pick over the pile to find the straightest knot-free stock I can, and let it go at that.

When I get my selections home, and cut them into frame stock, I examine the grain patterns with some care. For frames in the after sections of a boat, I choose stock with the straightest grain lengthwise, with the end grain running parallel to the planking of the boat. In the boat we're building in these pages, the frames nearest the transom require the best grain because they must take the hardest bends. These frames also have to be considerably overbent, because they just love to straighten out after they've been bent. Save the wood with the very best grain for the frames in this area.

When I made the half-model of this hull, I kept the framing very much in mind while I was shaping the quarter or stern corner right at the turn of the bilge. For stability, I wanted to keep the turn as hard as possible, but at the same time I wanted the frames to be able to take the bend without breaking. I had no magic formula—it was just a guesstimate. The frames made the

bend, but I think that if the turn had been a little sharper they might not have.

When you bend frames, you're asking wood to go in two directions: the bend on the inside of the stock compresses the grain, and the bend on the outside stretches it. You have to get the pulpy part of the wood structure soft enough, by steaming or boiling, to enable the grain layers to slip by one another.

I made my steam box from wood, and it was a little longer than the longest frame piece I would have to bend to achieve the curve demanded by half the greatest girth of the hull. Dowels running through holes in the box effectively kept the frame pieces separated, so that they would be exposed to steam evenly all around. A Coleman stove provided the heat, and a five-gallon can held the water. A piece of plastic pipe, pushed down over the spout of the can and leading into the after end of the box, fed steam into the chamber.

I set this rig up in my shop braced alongside a stanchion, with the steam-intake end elevated above the other; a bucket under the lower end caught the water that was condensed from the steam as it ran out.

The smaller the amount of water, the sooner it boils; I cut it pretty close, using as little as I thought I could get away with. Once in a while I ran dry, but since it was easy to tell when the steam stopped, nothing in this set-up ever got ruined.

To start with, put a dozen or so frames in the steam box and cover the steam intake with a thick cloth or any other material that will keep steam from leaking out. After about twenty minutes of making steam, pull out one frame and test its bendability on the floor. If it seems too stiff, give it about another ten minutes of steam.

Because green oak takes steam better than dry, I always got my bending stock as green as I could, right from the mill saw.

Framing calls for fast teamwork by two people, with one passing hot frames to the other, who stands in the boat skeleton and bends them into place. Both must wear heat-resistant gloves. The bender heels one end of

END GRAIN PARALLEL to the PLANKING

Planking

frame

STRAIGHT GRAIN

Grain of the frames.

the frame down on the keel and treads down with his other foot on the middle of the frame to crowd it into the sharpest bend at the turn of the bilge. At the same time, he pulls back on the top of the frame to overbend it, thus offsetting its tendency to straighten out. He bends the frame as far as he can without breaking it.

When each frame has been bent into place, its inboard end is nailed to the keel with inch-and-a-half Everdur boat nails, and the top end is tapped down snug against the ribbands. The frame should be clamped to at least one ribband, and fastened to the ribbands with five-penny galvanized nails. No drilling is necessary; when the wood is thoroughly steamed, you can nail through the frames, even close to the end, without any splitting.

You *can* do this entire framing process alone: I've framed a dozen or so carvel-planked hulls solo, in fact I've done most of them that way, but to do it is a full day's work. I'm not antisocial, but working alone has fewer complications. Then, too, my boat-building adrenalin won't allow me to just stand there waiting for somebody to get a piece ready and hand it to me. Call it a character defect.

Whether you do your framing by yourself, or with a helper, there are two things to watch for when bending in frames, and you'll encounter both of them.

The first is the danger of walking the ribbands off the molds in the flat sections of the hull—that is, to spring them away from the molds by your foot pressure when you're treading them into the sharp bends. The frames must be in pairs, port and starboard, to equalize pressure on this skeleton structure of the boat. Each such pair exerts a strong downward pressure on the ribbands, and especially from amidships aft when you're using foot pressure to crowd the frames down into place.

To counter this, you must shore up the ribbands with short uprights secured by nails to both the ribbands and the shop floor. Tilt the tops of these uprights inboard a little, and stagger them, so that your foot pressure will bear straight onto the uprights to keep them from kicking out sideways.

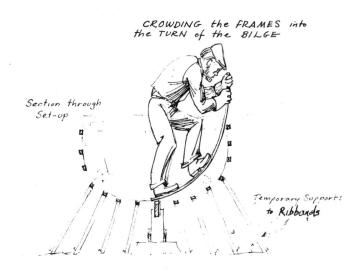

CROWDING the FRAMES into the TURN of the BILGE

Section through Set-up

Temporary Supports to Ribbands

NAILING the INBOARD END of the FRAME to the KEEL & CLAMPING the FRAME to a RIBBAND

Section through Set-up

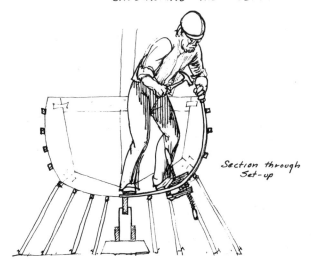

TAPPING the TOP END of the FRAME SNUG AGAINST the RIBBANDS

Section through Set-up

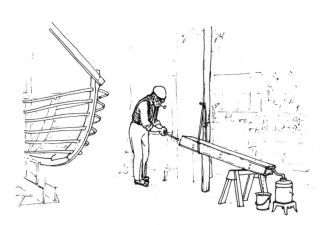

Steaming the frames.

Framing.

25

The second problem is that, having put your first pair of frames in at the midships station, running neatly straight across the width of the hull, you'll find that the rest of the frames fore and aft of amidships will begin to fight like hell against lying neatly in place that way.

This tendency for the frames to skew will show up quickly as soon as you have a few pairs in place. You'll begin to see that although the frames are spaced evenly at the centerline of the keel, they are not quite so evenly spaced along the sides of the boat. The reason for this is that the distance around the girth of the boat is greater than the distance down the length of the keel. To make up for this difference, you have to space the frames further apart at the sheerline. Pretty soon you will say to hell with perfection, and start swinging the frames a little so that they will lie comfortably along the inner skin of the hull.

Don't worry, there is no loss of structural strength from this. I can see that Alton Whitmore swung his frames, too; and although this practice may be avoidable, I've never seen any evidence that it is. My guess is that if such perfection could be achieved, it wouldn't be worth the trouble. I can tell you one thing for sure: you won't stand there long with a hot frame in your hands—gloves or no gloves—before you decide just where and how to install it.

Now she's all framed out. In the big old-time wooden ship-building yards, this was one of the stages when all hands knocked off for grog. That's optional.

You might think the floor timbers—the horizontal pieces between the frames—would be installed next, but they have to wait for the planking. Instead, the stopwaters are coming up on your timetable now.

With this particular set-up, you must drive two stopwaters—one at the forefoot joint and the other just aft of that at the keel joint. They must be driven now, before the planking covers these two joints.

The function of a stopwater is to keep the sea from following a joint and seeping through it into the boat. To install them, you bore holes right through the joints, cutting into both pieces of wood along the thwartship axis of the joints. Then you drive a snug pine plug dipped into white lead right through each hole, and cut it off flush with the rabbet line on both sides of the hull.

If you should happen to forget the stopwaters until after you've planked the hull, bore right through the planks and all, centering your drill so as to bore right through the joints on your way. There's no harm done, except to your pride if somebody notices the stopwaters showing through the paint.

Finishing off the framing was always a pleasant event for me, with or without grog. I would take time to walk around the hull and check the symmetry of the job from every angle. There was another pleasure involved: I could now go on to the planking, which is the job I came to enjoy most of all once I had planked my first boat and knew how.

10 Planking Her Up

I'm going to go through the planking process just as I did the first time around. I profited from my mistakes, and now I'm turning them over to you so you can do the same.

CHOOSING WOOD

Choosing the wood for planking a boat seems a simple enough process, unless you travel all over the country and find out all the varieties people use and why. The choice in my area is relatively simple. When I first nosed around to see what other people were using, I found that most of the builders in the Friendship shops used white pine—probably because at that time it was available in long lengths and good widths, and was relatively knot-free. At the same time, in the Rockland area, only a couple of dozen miles away, I never saw any builder use anything for planking but native cedar, unless a prospective owner specified otherwise.

Today, many an expensive yacht is planked with cedar. I settled for the local Maine variety a long time ago

and have planked all of my carvel-built boats with it.

Cedar has a lot going for it. It's lighter than pine, it cuts and planes nicely, and it bends well. I have no proof to back this, but I think it also swells and shrinks less than pine does. I know it holds paint better. Finally, it's available in relatively long lengths. In fact, if it weren't for its occasional knots and stretches of gray rot, I would say that cedar is the perfect wood for planking. And you can work around those two defects with very little trouble. The trick to planking with cedar is to buy about twice as much as you think you'll need.

How much do you need?

Simply figure the greatest girth of your boat, multiply this number by the overall length, and double the result. Don't worry about the taper of the hull shape. Your boat measures four feet from the keel to the sheer amidships, and the length is sixteen feet. Multiplying 16 by 8 gives you 128. Double that and you get 256 board feet. I would order 300.

Back when I built this particular boat, cedar was

going for twelve or thirteen cents a foot. Today it runs about forty-five cents, still a good buy when you compare it to Philippine mahogany, which is climbing over the two-dollar mark as I write. But mahogany is a wood I would never use anyway, since I am somehow allergic to its sawdust. For that matter, I know one prominent east-coast builder who after many years has had to give up working with cedar because he developed an allergy to it. Fortunately, such reactions are pretty rare, but no matter what virtues a species of wood has, you can't build boats with it if it makes you sick.

Much has changed in the past twenty-five years. When I bought cedar from Bill Munroe at Lincolnville Beach, he sawed it out just the way I wanted it, planed it to the thickness I specified, and delivered it, all for a reasonable price.

Today, no one is interested in selling small amounts of cedar to anyone. If I were to go to Lincolnville now and find any of the wood I wanted at all, it would be in stacks of a thousand board feet or so, all done up with metal bands. You can't pick over a pile like that.

I was always quite fussy about the lumber I picked. For the turn of the bilge, where the planks have to be hollowed out an eighth-inch or so, I'd have the planks planed to three-quarters of an inch instead of five eighths like the rest. Since about five-eighths of an inch would still be left after hollowing, the planking was approximately the same thickness throughout. Some builders don't bother with this allowance, and they don't have to if the turn of the bilge isn't too sharp. But I was using the boats I built and it was my neck that was at stake, so I didn't slight anything. I had the same respect for my customers' boats, too, I hasten to add.

GETTING THE GARBOARD RIGHT

With planking stock in hand, getting the garboard in was my top priority. First, however, I had to determine the several plank widths I would need. Obviously, if I wasn't careful how I laid off the planks, the planking on the sharp end of the boat was going to build up higher than the middle and the stern.

So I took my steel pocket rule and measured the girth from the keel to the sheer at the transom, again at the middle mold, and again at station number 1, and I wrote the figure down for each of these points.

Next, I divided these measurements into plank widths. At the midpoint, the distance from the keel to the sheer was forty-four inches, so there I needed eleven four-inch-wide planks to reach the sheer. At the transom, the distance was slightly less, and at the station number 1 mold it was about thirty-eight inches. I divided both these distances by eleven—for certainly I was going to have the same number of planks all along the side of my hull—to get the plank widths to accommodate each point.

To find the general shape of the garboard plank, I measured off those widths out from the keel on the corresponding molds at the three stations, marking each one on its mold. Then I bent a half-inch square batten from the stem rabbet to the transom, based on these three points.

I didn't know exactly where I wanted the top of the garboard to land in the stem rabbet, but when I sprung the batten around the three points in a fair curve, it showed me.

MEASURE from KEEL to SHEER
inside the RIBBANDS

Figuring out plank widths.

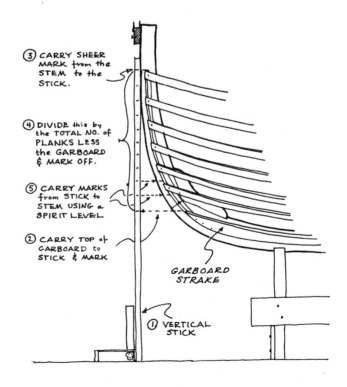

③ CARRY SHEER MARK from the STEM to the STICK.

④ DIVIDE this by the TOTAL NO. of PLANKS LESS the GARBOARD & MARK OFF.

⑤ CARRY MARKS from STICK to STEM USING a SPIRIT LEVEL

② CARRY TOP of GARBOARD to STICK & MARK

GARBOARD STRAKE

① VERTICAL STICK

Plank widths at the stem.

You can't measure up along the stem to mark off plank widths because the stem is raked. Therefore, to get these widths, hold your rule so that it extends vertically from the stem rabbet at the sheer and measure from this point down to where your batten has told you the top of the garboard plank will lie. Now divide that distance by ten—the number of planks remaining in addition to the garboard—and transfer these equal widths to the stem rabbet. Since you have to measure from a little way off the stem, you will have to use a level to make sure of marking these widths accurately.

You won't have to follow these marks exactly, but by having them clearly indicated you can guard against suddenly discovering that you have to work in a wider or a narrower plank to fill a space. Not that varying widths matter, structurally; planking all the way from the garboard to the sheer is all that really matters. But if you can make the lay of the planking pleasing to the eye, then why not?

When you use this system of planking by even divisions, you are locked in to equal plank widths at any given point all along the hull; however, that's not bad in itself. In fact, the practice is good for the beginner. On the other hand, running various shapes and widths of strakes wouldn't bother the pro one bit. But in the end you will benefit from this self-imposed discipline.

I was still in a quandary about getting the shape of the garboard. There was little to worry about from a bit forward of amidships to aft to the transom, because that area was so flat that planking it was almost as simple as boarding up a house. What bothered me was the twisty part of the hull up forward, where the garboard had to turn up and lie almost vertically against the stem rabbet. For a moment I gave serious thought to eyeballing it. Then I tried to recall what I knew, by hearsay, of lining out the shape with a spiling batten, but finally I decided to follow my old rule: *If you don't know, ask somebody who does.*

I picked out two friends: Walter Post, with whom I had fished off Metinic, and Maurice Sawyer, a longtime boat-builder at Morse's yard in Thomaston, where he was one of their best adze men. They both showed me how they used a three-eighths-inch-by-three-inches-by-sixteen-foot spiling batten, marking it off with a pair of dividers locked at a certain setting with one leg on the rabbet line and the other on the batten. The idea was to make a series of marks along the batten, remove the batten from the boat and lay it on a plank, transfer the marks to the plank, drive in a nail at each mark, and sweep in the cut line with another batten. All you had to do then was saw the plank to the line.

When I'd done all this, however, the plank didn't fit.

Looking back later, I could think of several factors that might have led to my failure. Both the men who showed me the technique were used to working on large hulls, where you don't get so much twist in a single plank. Another possibility was that when I made the cut in the plank, the grain tension was released and that made the plank go out of true. This happens quite often: you make a template for some hard-to-fit piece, use it for a pattern, and find that the result doesn't fit

worth a hoot, all because of released grain stress.

Whatever the reason for my garboard plank's failure to fit snugly into its rabbet, my friends had disappeared without solving the mystery. I decided to forget spiling for the time being and make a template.

I cut a piece of quarter-inch plywood long enough to extend back into the flat section of the body and still reach the stem. I then shoved one end as far as I could into the rabbet, clamped it in tight against the frames and the rabbet line of the keel, and scribed the forward end as best I could. Next, I traced around my plywood template directly onto the forward end of a piece of planking and sawed to the cutline.

When I put the plank in, I didn't dare use enough clamp pressure to twist it into place cold; instead, I gave it the steam-bath treatment. With this, it went right into place, and so did its mate on the other side.

The number-one plank was next, though, and I still didn't know how to spile. Nor was I going to make a template for every plank. Finally it dawned on me: why not take a plank and wrap it around the garboard, with its lower edge down over the top of the garboard, and trace around the top edge of the garboard right onto the second plank? It would have to fit, and it did.

Years later I read of this as a recommended substitute for spiling. I think it offers important advantages of its own. It's a little faster than spiling because you don't have to transfer measurements from a spiling batten to the plank. Also, it helps train your eye to select the right plank to use in a given location—a plank that will have the right curve in it. And believe me, when you have developed an educated eye, you will have a tremendous asset.

BEVELS AND HOLLOWS

You will find little need for hollowing your first few planks or strakes. However, you will find this necessary for some of the later planks. Beveling comes first. To see why your plank edges will have to be planed to a slight angle to let them be closely fitted, just think of a barrel and the edge-angles of its staves, or consider the sections of an orange.

For beveling, you'll need a small bevel square. A car-

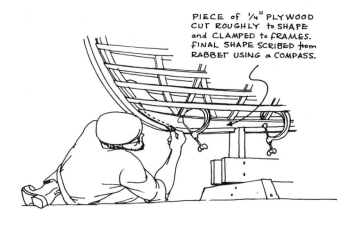

PIECE of ¼" PLYWOOD
CUT ROUGHLY to SHAPE
and CLAMPED to FRAMES.
FINAL SHAPE SCRIBED from
RABBET USING a COMPASS.

Garboard template.

penter's square is too big to use for this work, so you will have to make your own or adapt some other tool. I happen to have a mechanic's point-setting gauge, with one arm about three inches long and the other a trifle shorter, and it works just right.

The greatest planking bevels are required near the stern, when you are planking the turn of the bilge; as you move forward they decrease steadily until you have no bevel at all at the stem. Use your bevel square to take the bevel angle from the top of the last plank you have fastened in place, and transfer this bevel to the bottom of the next plank. To do this, put the arm or handle of the square against the frame at the same angle at which the plank is going to lie, and swing the blade down until it lies flat across the edge of the preceding plank. Then apply the square to the bottom of the up-coming plank, deciding which side will be outside the hull and which inside, and whittle out a segment of the plank until the blade fits flat across it. Continue this process along the whole length of the plank, at whatever intervals you decide are necessary. Then, with the plank in your vise, plane down to all the marks and connect them in a fair and gradual curve.

If you doubt your ability to do this by eye alone, then fair the marks with a batten first.

What you are trying for is a wood-to-wood joint between the inboard edges of the planking. After the plank has been beveled and put in place, you may find places where the outside edges of the two planks are also wood to wood. The plank must then be taken off and the outside edge planed at a slight bevel in those areas to open them enough to accept caulking. Or, if you wish, you can ignore these tight spots for the time being, and open them later with a seam-reefing tool. In any case, before you put the plank in place plane the caulking seam very lightly.

I use a fifteen-inch wooden jackplane with a screw-adjusted cutting iron for my beveling. It's the only wooden-bodied jackplane with a screw adjustment that I have seen, and I will never part with it. It works much more smoothly than an iron plane, without any drag whatsoever. For dressing the bevel, I also use a small low-angle block plane.

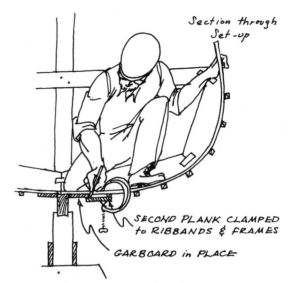

SECOND PLANK CLAMPED to RIBBANDS & FRAMES

GARBOARD in PLACE

Section through Set-up

Taking the shape of the second plate.

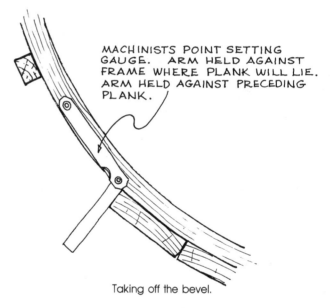

MACHINISTS POINT SETTING GAUGE. ARM HELD AGAINST FRAME WHERE PLANK WILL LIE. ARM HELD AGAINST PRECEDING PLANK.

Taking off the bevel.

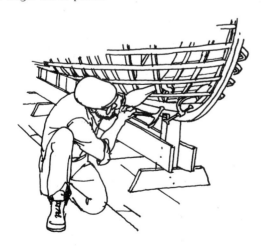

Fitting the garboard.

BOTTOM of PLANK

INSIDE of PLANK

Transferring the bevel.

You will first discover the need for hollowing in the bow area, where your planks are beginning to cross frames that have some bends in them; you'll see that the plank edges on the flat side don't touch the frame, and you must hollow the backs of these planks so they will fit snugly against the frames.

You will need at least one hollowing plane for this work; if you have two—one with less radius than the other—all the better. You will need the latter for the forward portions of your planks, because you will be removing less wood, in accordance with the less-pronounced bends in the frames in the forward area.

Both of my hollowing planes are eight inches long, and both are made of a very hard wood, with the name "J. Doyle" stamped on the ends. Undoubtedly, Mr. Doyle was a boat-builder from long ago, and is now deceased. I hope the name rings a bell with someone, for I would dearly love to see some of the boats J. Doyle's planes have helped shape. I've had the planes for over a quarter of a century, doing my share of boat-building with them. Soon they will pass to the next generation.

You will need a guide for your hollowing. From your planking, or from scrap stock, cut a length equal to the greatest width of the planking. On it, trace the curve of the frame with the strongest bend, and saw out the wood along your trace line. This is your pattern—a template for that particular spot. Now cut another template for the frame closest to amidships, and you can get on with your hollowing. Working forward from the transom, start hollowing in the center of each plank, using your plane with the greatest radius; work outward, with lighter cuts toward the edges, all the while trying your template for fit. Be very careful not to knock the edges off the plank. When you've reached amidships, switch to the plane with the shallower radius.

Eye, hand, and template are your guides when hollowing planks. The work is not difficult, but it is tedious. Early during my first attempt at hollowing, I noticed that if I put a straightedge across some of my planking stock, one side showed an inherent hollowness and the other had a corresponding convexity. This is caused by the drying of the wood. The hollows are always from the heart of the tree, in the direction opposite to the annular growth rings which makes planing easier. When the plank is in place, the cup side, in terms of the annular rings, is outboard.

I took advantage of this when I could. However, I found that because of the way the stick comes off the mill saw, the heart of the wood will lie off to one side up to the middle of the plank and off to the other side from the middle to the end.

If you're as fussy as I am, after you have finished planing the hollow take some coarse sandpaper, say 60 grit, on a piece of wood shaped to match your greatest-curve template, and sand the inside of the hollow.

I always found that installing a pair of strakes at the turn of the bilge was a full day's work.

FASTENINGS

The first carvel-planked boats I built were clench-nailed with wedge-point galvanized nails. With their protruding points clenched—that is, turned over and driven back into the frame they had been driven through—these nails provided strong construction. However, I sometimes made the beginner's classic mistake of splitting the hood end of a plank by lining up one of those chisel points with the grain. The points of wedge-point nails must always be aligned so that they cut across the grain.

I changed to silicon-bronze anchor-type ringed nails as soon as they came on the market. They are easier to use and don't have to be driven clear through the frames to give holding power. This characteristic makes for a much better-looking planking job.

For planking, I use inch-and-one-eighth number 13 wire in these anchor nails; this size is long enough to be buried in, but not go through, the frames. I pre-bore for them with a five-sixty-fourths-inch bit, and set the heads by driving them in a little with a punch. I used three fastenings at the hood end of each plank and two at each frame. I have never had a single plank pull away from a frame.

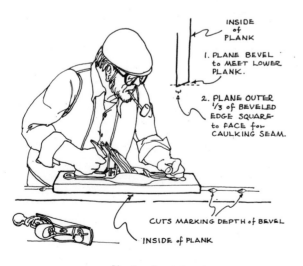

Planing the edge.

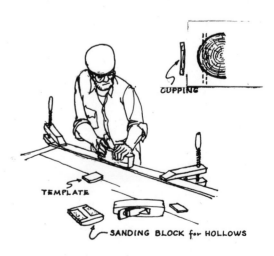

Hollowing.

When planking, my practice has always been to start with the garboards and work up to the sheer. Plenty of boats are planked in both directions, with a shutter plank used to close them up. I didn't use this method, primarily because I knew that my framing wasn't any too precise. If you don't achieve the exact shape of the hull with your bent frames, and you put the sheer strake on first, and plank down toward the keel, you will lock in any irregularities that may have been introduced. (On large boats, however, a little skilled adze work will take care of frame irregularities, and planking in both directions is possible, and makes sense because two planking teams can work at the same time.) Futhermore, when you plank a small boat from the keel up, the hull has a way of fairing itself; the planks are free to adjust themselves because with no "roof" over them, they have a little leeway to come and go.

One problem with planking is that bent frames like to straighten out a little, especially in the after part of the hull. Before I realized how much overbending was needed to offset this, I would often find myself looking along the planking from the stern to the first mold and seeing hollows in what should have been the smooth skin of the boat there. To fix these, I had to cut cross-palls and wedge them down between the planking and the frames. By hammering the tops of the crosspalls down, I could get the line fair again.

So it goes. You learn a little here and a little there, and pretty soon you've built your first boat and are ready to tackle the next one with more confidence and ease.

"THOU SHALT NOT EDGE-SET"

Edge-setting is pounding down on a plank to make it fit tightly against the one below, when it doesn't quite want to naturally. I'd heard stern warnings against doing this so often and for so many years that they had come to sound like biblical commands to me. But if such a practice is truly a sin, then I am certainly Hell-bound, because I have yet to see a single plank I didn't have to edge-set a little. Still, it bothered my conscience, and I wondered how much I could get away with without endangering my boat-builder's soul.

One day while prowling around the Rockland Boat Shop looking for God knows what, I saw a perfectly respectable-looking workman edge-setting the daylights out of one of the uppermost strakes of the hull he was working on. Between strokes of his hammer I hollered, "I thought that was a no-no!"

He knew what I meant. He hollered right back over the noise of the shop, "We don't waste any wood around here! The boss always says to get all you can out of that stick."

I never worried about edge-setting one bit after that. I saw that the men in that shop even had a special tool for edge-setting, which they called a gusset or a triangle. And when I saw how effective their little gadget was, and how simple it was to make, I made up a set for myself.

But don't get me wrong—there are limits. If you happen to saw a quick place in the plank, say a departure

Pre-boring for nails.

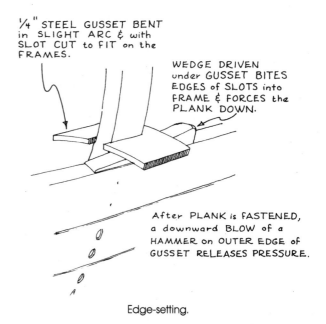

¼" STEEL GUSSET BENT in SLIGHT ARC & with SLOT CUT to FIT on the FRAMES.

WEDGE DRIVEN under GUSSET BITES EDGES of SLOTS into FRAME & FORCES the PLANK DOWN.

After PLANK is FASTENED, a downward BLOW of a HAMMER on OUTER EDGE of GUSSET RELEASES PRESSURE.

Edge-setting.

of a quarter-inch or more from the true line within a space of two feet, don't try edge-setting. If you have lined off your planks carefully, either by the wrap-around or the spiling batten method, there is no reason not to edge-set them in place. I always laid off the top edge of every plank with a batten to establish a fair curve, which was my insurance that the next plank set to it was going to have an acceptable fit. Some boat-builders have assured me that they always line off each plank by eye, but I was happy enough to stick to my method since it worked for me.

Those edge-setting gussets are simple to make and use, but difficult to explain; I recommend that you consult the drawing of one of them. Each one is made of quarter- or five-sixteenths-inch steel plate measuring two and a half by three inches. In the center of the three-inch side, a slot is cut out; this exactly accommodates the frame when, as you stand outside the hull, you slide the gusset over the frame of the plank you are attempting to set down. There is also a slight bend in the gusset, about an eighth- or quarter-inch in radius, running crossways to the planking. With the gusset in place, a wedge is driven between the planking and the frame right under the gusset and running fore and aft. When this wedging force is applied, the curve in the gusset makes the sides of the slot bite into the frame and provide purchase. The harder you drive the wedge, the firmer the grip of the gusset on the frame. Half a dozen of these gadgets all doing their job can bring your planks together in a hurry. When the plank in question has been fastened to the frame, a downward blow of a hammer quickly releases the gusset.

The gussets cost almost nothing to make and are far ahead of anything you can buy. You can't beat that combination.

I hadn't done much planking before I noticed that most of my clamps couldn't reach down to the bottom edge of a four-inch-wide plank. This was because they were not true C-clamps but were made straight across in the jaws. You can get true C-clamps, which are actually shaped like the letter C, and I advise you to do so because they work fine in difficult places.

KEEPING YOUR HOOD ENDS UP

Hood ends are the extreme forward ends of the planks, where they are fitted to the stem rabbet. As your planking progresses, these hood ends will tend to hook down. This does no harm, in utilitarian terms, but it will spoil the looks of your planking if you let it continue. This droop in the hood ends is the natural result of the twisting that occurs as a plank shifts toward a nearly vertical attitude as it approaches the stem. If you see the hood ends beginning to droop as you study your hull in profile, start making each successive hood end a little wider, if the space allows, or making the planks a little narrower where the top of the downturn curve comes. All you have to do is shift the batten a little when you're lining off the top edge of each plank.

Another place to keep your eye peeled for the appearance of an unsightly hump is in the after part of the sheer, where the stern has some tumblehome—that is, the sides of the hull curve gently inward from the widest beam aft to the slightly narrower beam at the sheer; they tend to "tumble home." As the sheer strake twists from perhaps a little flare amidships to roll slightly inboard on the top at the stern, a droop or hump may show up. You can correct this in the same way you avoided the drooping hood-end effect.

THE SPECIAL PLEASURES OF PLANKING

I was fearful of planking my first boat, but when the mystery of the job disappeared, planking became the work I enjoyed most. I finally realized that there was only so much space to be filled, and that if I let it, my batten would show me the right way to fill it.

Of all the false conceptions I had about planking, the most burdensome was my conviction that some hocus-pocus was involved—that the shape of each plank had to be figured out by a method that was understood only by a master builder who lived right. That idea faded and then disappeared with each plank that I laid out and fastened in place. As I watched the batten show me the way, I soon came to understand the simple secrets of planking.

Near the garboard, the edges of the planks had an outside curve, which gradually diminished as the planks rose to the bilge, and finally leveled out to lie straight along the turn of the bilge. Yet, when I passed that point and started up toward the sheer, strange things seemed to happen: when I put my batten to the plank widths that showed there was just so much space left, the batten, instead of following a nice fair curve, started to assume an S shape akin to a snake's path.

If I hadn't succeeded by trusting the batten up to that point, I would have had grave doubts about what it was telling me now. But I had begun to see that arguing with my batten was about as productive as arguing with my compass, and long ago I had learned that that was a fool's game. So I stopped paying attention to the batten as I thought it should look and concentrated instead on how it actually did look. And I reached the sheer of that boat with a planking job I was proud to claim as mine. Never before nor since have I done anything that pleased me more.

In discussing planking up so far, I've left out a few things; I wanted to get the overall technique without a cluttering of fine details. Now let's catch up with some of those points.

For example, I learned that the forward ends of planks that require steaming should be put in the stem rabbet first and clamped in place while they're hot. This way you have the whole length of the plank to give you twisting leverage. Trying to twist the forward ends into the stem rabbet last, after I had clamped the after part in place, cost me quite a few unsuccessful trials before it dawned on me that I was going at it backwards. Chalk that one up to the learning process.

Then there's the matter of butt joints. Most people think there are butt joints in the planking of every boat. However, all the boats I have built were planked with full-length strakes—with one exception, caused by the cracking of one plank after it had been fastened. I think butt joints are unsightly, and they are also prone to rot, and I advise you to avoid them as I do. Keep the strakes to a maximum width of four inches, and you'll be able to use full-length planking stock, especially in a hull shape which is wider aft and narrow forward. Such a hull is suited to the natural shape of live-edge boards, and you'll have very little waste in your planking wood.

If for any reason you do have to use butt joints, stagger them at least three or four planks apart, and never let them fall in the same frame space as another butt in any other plank. When you saw the two pieces of plank that are to be butted, make the cuts at a slight angle; the joints will close tighter if they are diagonal. Every such joint must be backed up by a butt block—a short length of planking stock that covers the joint on the inner side of the butted planks and is securely nailed and glued to both of them, functioning somewhat like a splint. The corners of the butt blocks must be angled or rounded off to facilitate drainage of any water that may collect on them.

As I learned later by experimentation, when I built this same hull over again, paper patterns work very well in determining the shape of individual planks. I used building paper to make patterns for eight of the eleven planks needed on each side of the hull, and tucked them away for future reference. Later, when I lent the molds and set-up for the boat to Carl Ilvonen, my brother-in-law, and Ronald Anderson, they simply unrolled the paper patterns, placed them on the planks, traced around them, and cut to the lines. The planks fitted exactly. What a time saver!

The reason I didn't make patterns of the other three planks was to permit enough leeway for changing their shapes if another builder decided on a slightly different sheer.

When you use thicker planking to allow for hollowing along the turn of the bilge, keep in mind that you must set the nail heads deeper; if you don't, you'll be sorry when the time comes to plane the hull for smoothing.

As you plank more boats, your skill will improve and so will the appearance of your finished product. One refinement is to make the sheer strake wider than the rest. Then, when a gunwale is sprung around the sheer strake, the uncovered portion of this strake will appear to be about the same width as the other lower strakes. However, while this is a fine touch for a yacht, for a working fishing boat it's a detail I would never bother with.

My record time for building a small carvel-planked boat was twenty-two days—that was in the month of June, when I didn't have to tend my wood stove. When you get to the sheer strake of your first hull and are gloating over the lovely planking job you're so justly proud of, you're just about half done, for it will take about the same length of time to finish your boat and have her ready for the water.

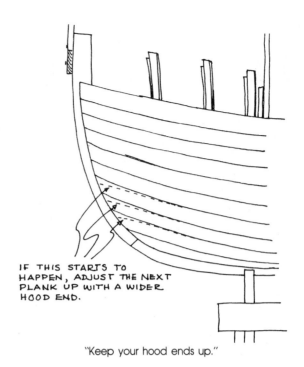

IF THIS STARTS TO HAPPEN, ADJUST THE NEXT PLANK UP WITH A WIDER HOOD END.

"Keep your hood ends up."

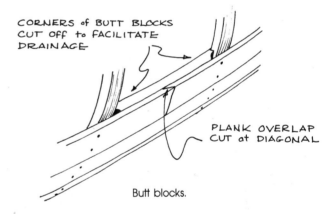

CORNERS of BUTT BLOCKS CUT OFF to FACILITATE DRAINAGE

PLANK OVERLAP CUT at DIAGONAL

Butt blocks.

Paper patterns of the garboard and the next seven planks, with last three planks omitted to allow builders and customers a choice of sheer and looks. (Photo by the author.)

11 Finishing Off

This chapter covers a multitude of opportunities for sinning against the soundness of your boat or its usability. Before I get into them, I should discuss the use of both galvanized and bronze fastenings in one hull which I've recommended. Will electrolysis make the bronze eat the galvanized bolts, or perhaps vice versa?

I've been accused of, and have even been detected, doing strange things. One cold blustery day while crossing the channel, I took the garbage can cover from my bait tub and held the thing in front of my face to ward off the ice spray. For that, for a while, I earned the nickname "Gladiator." One summer, tired of squinting all day against too much sun, I installed a polka-dot umbrella in my center thwart, after which my fishing friends in other boats indulged in such feeble jokes as "Make mine with mustard." But none of that bothered me because I was concerned with a possible potential danger I couldn't see: the threat of electrolytic action from using mixed metals in salt water. Had I constructed a battleground for a war to the death among my own fastenings? I couldn't tell for sure, but I wasn't going to the extreme of cutting up a perfectly sound boat to find out.

I found out twenty years later, after a bizarre accident. At the end of a season's fishing, I was trailering my boat home for winter storage. I felt a bump with a difference, and when I braked the truck to slow down, the boat and the trailer passed quite properly on the left and then veered off the road to take down my neighbor's mailbox and bury the trailer's tongue out of sight in his stone wall. Whereupon a skiff that was riding piggyback in the bigger boat slid forward and split the bigger boat, wedging its bow open all the way down to the keel.

I won't pretend that the first thing I did was inspect the fastenings for electrolytic damage. Not until months later—after several occasions when I almost adopted my friends' advice to burn the damn thing (although I later put it back together again instead)—did I take a good look at them. The bronze was fine, and there was only minute deterioration of the galvanized keel and stem-knee bolts. Pretty good condition after twenty years' service.

Larger, heavily powered boats, I've heard again and again, aren't that lucky when mixed metal fastenings are used. At times two vessels with incompatible fastenings even make an electrolytic cannibal feast of one another when they're moored close together.

I did have some trouble from electrolysis with a twenty-six-footer of mine. One year after I had installed a protective cage over the propeller with half-inch stainless steel lag screws, I hauled the boat out and found that these fastenings looked like rotten teeth. I replaced them with monel screws and never had any more trouble, although I wondered at the time whether I had merely switched the potential threat to galvanized fastenings elsewhere on that hull.

Back to the boat.

FLOOR TIMBERS

In the type of hull we're building, the floor timbers are not the edgewise verticals, perpendicular to the keel and at right angles to it, that are adjoined to the frames in some larger boats. They are merely wood strips bent against, and fastened to, the planking between the frames. They add necessary stiffness to the hull because they extend across the bottom instead of being butted on the centerline as the frames are.

Before you put the floor timbers in, cross-brace the hull at the sheer and then remove the molds. The cross-bracing is temporary; all that is required is a few spreaders which can be held in place athwartships with clamps, or lightly nailed; you can putty or plug the nail holes later. Without this bracing, the sides will tend to cave in at the top. One of the first boats I ever planked took on the shape of a cigar at the top because I hadn't thought to brace her off before removing the molds.

Two-inch-wide-by-three-quarter-inch-thick oak strips will do for floor timbers. Cut as many as you will need to put one between each pair of frames, all the way from the transom to the deadwood on the after part of the forefoot. They should be about two and a half feet long at the transom and gradually become shorter as you approach the stem. The planking line can serve as a rough guide for laying them down.

Steam each floor timber before you set them in, so there won't be any pressure from their ends pushing against the planking as there would be if you forced them in cold.

To fasten a floor timber, first put it in place, trace around it, and take it out. Next, bore through the hull planking from the inside, exactly where you want your fastenings to go. Then put the timber back in place, and fasten it at the centerline of the keel with a boatnail, either galvanized or bronze, or a screw if you prefer. With a helper inside the hull holding a maul against the floor timber to back the nails for you, from the outside fasten the planking to the timber using the same nails as you used for the planking of the hull.

CUTTING DOWN THE TRANSOM

Your outboard motor requires a maximum transom height of from fifteen to fifteen and a half inches above the bottom of the boat for the standard short-shafted outboard rig. This calls for cutting out a section of the transom so that it will accept your motor, not only vertically but also horizontally to allow for the maximum swing of the motor as you steer. Because motor dimensions vary, the best way to arrive at the dimensions of your cutout is by trial and error, mounting the motor itself. If you don't have the motor at hand, apply your math, basing your computation on whatever motor dimensions you have available.

An outboard motor puts considerable bending strain on a transom, so the transom must be beefed up in the vicinity of the motor's screw clamps. Two vertical pieces of oak, about three inches wide and long enough to reach the top of the bottom transom framing, will be adequate. Fasten them with stout screws that won't project through the transom.

Let's assume that you want to camber your transom—give it a transverse curve ahtwartships that will carry right on through all the upperworks. Such a curve can be applied continuously as you work forward—in the breasthook, which is the abbreviated triangular decking right in the bow, for example, and in the gunwales. To make these curves you will need a crowning board—a template that you can slide along the entire length of the boat, from its widest to its narrowest dimension, and produce the proper transverse curve even for the gunwales at any point.

MAKING A CROWNING BOARD

The method I recommend for making a crowning board is derived from one by Sam Rabl, as described in his book *Boatbuilding in Your Own Backyard* (Cambridge, Mass.: Cornell Maritime Press, 1958). I've worked out crowning board curves by other techniques in my time, but when I tried this method on a boat called *Featherwind*, designed by Phil Bolger, I was convinced it was the simplest. *Featherwind* has an arched center thwart that serves two functions: it is pleasing to the eye, and when the boat is heeled over, it keeps the person sitting on the weather side from sliding down toward the lee gunwale. I used Rabl's foolproof method to build this thwart, and it worked beautifully.

The drawings will help explain the procedure. Begin with two sticks (laths will do), cross them near one end, and drive a nail through this point of intersection to make them into free-swing scissors. Choose any convenient length for these sticks, provided only that they are long enough to be manipulated according to the following instructions and still maintain an angular crossing. Next, measure the greatest width of the boat at the gunwale—including the thickness of the sheer plank—and lay that length out as a straight horizontal line on the board you are going to use as your template, or crowning board. Now drive a nail at each end of this straight line, determine the height of the crown you will want at the center of its arc amidships, and erect a vertical line of that height at the center of the horizontal line. Drive a nail at the top of this vertical.

Now rest each leg of your scissors on one of the end nails of your thwartships line and let the apex of the scissors hang on the maximum mid-arc height nail, and lock the scissors into this relationship by driving a second nail through both laths where they cross at the apex. Remove the nail that has been marking the arc's maximum height, and hold a pencil in its place. Now keep the pencil firmly in this position, and keep the two arms of the scissors always resting on and in close con-

CROSS-BRACING the HULL before REMOVING MOLD

Cross-spalls.

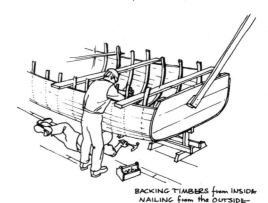

BACKING TIMBERS from INSIDE NAILING from the OUTSIDE

Floor timbers.

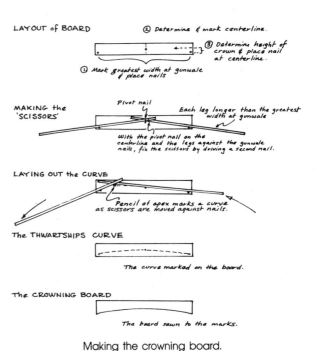

LAYOUT of BOARD　②Determine & mark centerline.
③Determine height of crown & place nail at centerline.
①Mark greatest width at gunwale & place nails

MAKING the 'SCISSORS'
Pivot nail
Each leg longer than the greatest width at gunwale
With the pivot nail on the centerline and the legs against the gunwale nails, fix the scissors by driving a second nail.

LAYING OUT the CURVE
Pencil at apex marks a curve as scissors are moved against nails.

The THWARTSHIPS CURVE
The curve marked on the board.

The CROWNING BOARD
The board sawn to the marks.

Making the crowning board.

tact with the other two nails. As you move the apex from one side to the other, letting the legs slide over their respective end nails, the pencil will draw a perfect arc. Saw to that line, and you will have your crowning board.

To use it on your transom, center the board on the transom with the arc cutting its outboard corners, and you will be able to trace the proper curve on either side of the gap you have cut to accommodate your outboard motor. You can use this same crowning board as a template for the thwartships curve of each sheer plank, each gunwale, and the breasthook in the bow.

I've used the phrase "center it" a number of times. I can't overstress the importance of centering everything. When I first started building, I didn't center things often enough, and I paid dearly for it in lost time. Whenever a centerline is called for, mark it on both sides and on the top and bottom of every piece of wood that's involved.

My father taught me the fastest way to find the center of anything: Guess at it first, then measure from one end, or edge, to your estimated center. Then measure the same distance from the opposite reference point, and divide the difference—either overlap or shortfall—in half. You'll be pleasantly surprised how good your eye can become at this. It's a method that certainly beats trying to divide feet, inches, and funny fractions.

When you try your new crowning board way up in the bow of your hull, you'll find that there is more than enough crown in the top of the planking already, because of the flare in the bows. You can just leave the crown there, and use the crowning board as a guide for carrying the proper arc all the way aft to the tumblehome.

SEAT RISERS, SEATS, AND KNEES

The longitudinals that run inside the frames to provide a base for the seats, or thwarts, of your boat don't have to extend the full length of the hull, although customarily they do. Either way you choose, a good piece of planking material is the best stock to use for these risers. Select stock that is three-quarters by one and three-quarters or two inches, showing good grain and free of knots. Risers are sometimes made of oak, but not by me; oak risers tend to rot, so I make mine from cedar. I fasten them on the flat to each frame, using one nail.

Seat or thwart locations are a matter of choice, depending to some degree on whether you will use the boat for work or for pleasure. I have put them in several ways. I used to install the stern seat snug up against the transom, but that location is awkwardly close to the motor, both for easy steering and because the motor has a habit of depositing an oil scum right there. Worse still, for me, was the ingenuity of the crabs that I occasionally found in my lobster traps and dumped into the boat. They invariably scuttled under the seat, where they provided interesting bare-handed groping.

I started placing the stern seats forward a little, and used two of them—one to port and one to starboard—for sidesaddle-style sitting. I made them hollow like

boxes, with lift-up tops so I could stow gear in them. I installed a crosswise thwart amidships, another forward of that, and still another in the bow.

For all thwarts, I suggest seven-eighths-inch spruce or oak, with a minimum width of nine and a half inches. Because most of the in-and-out flexing of the boat sides is amidships, I would certainly use at least seven-eighths stock there, even if you do use lighter stock elsewhere.

Thwarts must be fastened to the sides of the boat with knees of some sort—usually triangular pieces of wood, with the vertical edge fastened to the planking and the horizontal edge supporting, and fastened to, the thwart. My version will make the purists howl: I use half-inch copper pipe, placed at a 45° angle where the thwart meets the planking, with the ends pounded out flat to receive the fastenings. Copper-pipe knees have no grain to split, and when riveted through both the seat and the hull, they will last longer than the rest of the boat ever will.

Natural knees are great, but don't expect to find me running through the woods in search of them. Admittedly they are far superior to straight-grained wood for knees. No matter how careful you are about cutting in relation to the grain, you'll be wasting your time. Sooner or later all straight-grain knees will give up; I've replaced many that I put in myself.

If copper pipe turns your off, and you don't want to hunt for natural knees, then look for knee stock with knots—tough ones, the kind you would hesitate to split with an axe—and your boat will stand a chance of keeping her knees intact.

Without knees of some kind, your boat will develop middle-age spread over the years. Strangely enough, the boat that hit the stone wall did develop middle-age spread, but gained in looks because the accident changed her rather straight sheer into a rockered curve that was more pleasing to the eye. Each year she looks better—not a bad way to go.

The breasthook and the stern-quarter knees go in next, and here some very good builders admit that their shop stoves have consumed more than their share of failures, so take your time. You have ends to fit and side bevels and curves to contend with.

For the breasthook, which fills the triangle between the gunwales where they meet at the bow, I use two pieces of wood, each with its grain running along the curve of the gunwale, and joined down the centerline with a spline like that used in the transom, or doweled together and glued. I know this works, because old Alton Whitmore's breasthook is still in the boat I bought from him, and so are mine, done the same way, in a number of working hulls.

Your crowning board can take care of the transverse curve of the breasthook, and you can use it to establish the proper curve of the stern-quarter knees, too. To cut the quarter knees to the right bevel, place the crowning board across the top of the planking, and find the necessary bevel between the top plank and the horizontal knee. Cut notches in both stern-quarter knees to accept the inside gunwale, and fasten the knees to both the planking and the transom.

I have noticed that all the stern knees I have put in
have tended, in time, to work away from the transom
because the fastenings have been driven into the edge
grain there. This would not happen in a boat used only
for rowing, but the stress of an outboard motor will
eventually produce a crack in the grain. This can be
avoided, although at some expense in appearance, by
fastening the knee down to the top of the transom, or
fastening the knee to a cleat located on the inside of the
transom.

GUNWALES

To install the inside rail or gunwale, first use your
crowning board to establish the arc that will be required
for the rail top, entering marks at sufficient intervals—at
least one at each frame—along the full length of the
rail. Cut the gunwale from a piece of three-quarter-
inch-by-sixteen-foot oak, long enough to extend beyond
the bow when curved, and snap it into the notch you
have made in the stern-quarter knee. Bring this rail to
the marks you have made at each frame, and clamp it
in place.

The rail, or gunwale, will extend beyond the notch
you made in the breasthook. To cut it to the exact
length for a tight end fit forward, begin by placing your
rule against the breasthook notch where the end of the
rail will come, and extend the rule to where the gunwale is clamped against the forward frame. Hold the
rule tight against the inside top edge of the sheer strake,
so that it is lying against the frames just as the gunwale
will lie. Then swing the end of the rule from the breasthook notch onto the gunwale and mark where it
touches. When it has been cut off here, the rail will fit
exactly.

Cut your outside gunwale from one-and-a-quarter by
seven-eighths-inch oak. Bevel the bottom edge about
thirty degrees, or leave it square if you prefer. Now wrap
the gunwale along the side and clamp it in place. Using
a five-thirty-seconds counterbore, drill through the outside gunwale, the planking and the inside gunwale on
every frame. To fasten, drive a 9-penny flat head copper
nail through all three. Cut off the inside nail end with a
hacksaw, leaving enough protruding to slip a number 9
copper burr—a flat copper washer—over it, and then
upset the end (pound the end flat over the burr).

The counterbore offers the quickest way to drill for
the gunwale nails, since it bores both a small pilot hole
and a countersink that will accept a three-eighths-inch
bung, all in one pass. Counterbores may be available in
your local area; I've heard there is a hardware store in
midtown Manhattan where you can get them, and I'm
sure there are quite a few other sources scattered across
the country. If you're not near one, I recommend that
you order your counterbore from Rockland Boat Company, 23 Sea Street Place, Rockland, Maine 04841. In
business for more than half a century, this firm knows
boat-building needs first-hand and has all the fastenings
you might require—bronze screws, bronze anchor nails,
and the whole gamut of other hard-to-find items. The
company will accept mail orders—I made a point of
asking.

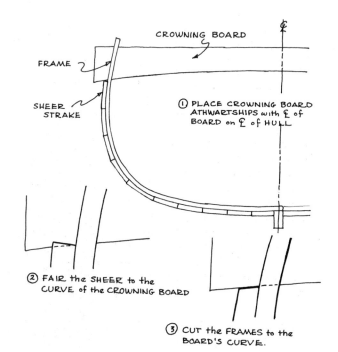

Using the crowning board.

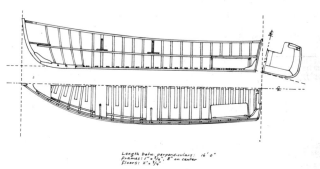

Construction drawing.

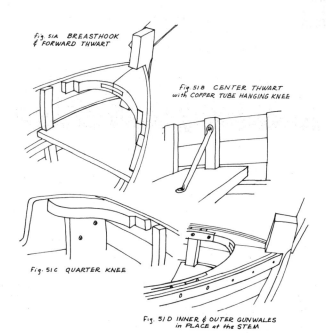

Seats, knees, etc.

You can skip the counterbore if you wish by boring your bunghole first and then boring the pilot hole, using two different bits, but this is a slow process.

While we're on the subject, there is another kind of counterbore I wouldn't be without. That's the Fuller combination countersink-counterbore. It handles screw pilot holes from numbers 6 to 14, and counterbores of three-eighths and one-half inch. It's good only for screws, because it has a short tapered drill, and it won't do for through fastenings, but it is more readily available than the straight counterbore.

With the gunwales fastened on both sides of your hull, fill the countersink holes with three-eighths-inch oak bungs dipped in glue, taking care that their grain runs with the grain of the outside rail. Cut the bungs off flush with a flat chisel—but don't try for a flush cut at the first whack, or you'll find that some of your bung surfaces will end up lower than the surface of the rail because of irregularities in the grain.

SMOOTHING AND CAULKING

Now turn your boat over and start planing the hull to achieve a smooth outer skin. On the flatter sections not much wood will have to be taken off, but at the turn of the bilge you'll have to work carefully with the plane, and sandpaper as well, to round her off.

Pine and mahogany planking aren't too touchy to sand, but cedar has very hard and sandpaper-resisting knots and it is easy to sand too deeply in the areas between the knots and produce an irregular surface. Only experience can tell you how much or how little to sand cedar; so, while you're gaining that experience, take it easy.

For caulking, one ball of cotton wicking will be enough for a boat of this size. Cotton wicking looks like kite string, only rougher and thicker.

You'll need three tools for caulking, two of which you can make. One is a reamer, sometimes called a "reefing tool," to open the seam where a seam is too tight and therefore must be widened (even experts misjudge bevels sometimes, and must use a reamer). I make my reamers from a flat ten-inch file. Simply bend the tang over at a right angle and cut off most of the end so that the remainder is just deep enough to reach into the seam; this provides better control. Grind the business end of the reamer into a wedge-shaped taper, rounded on the bottom and tapered fore and aft so that it will spread the seam without digging into the plank edges.

The second tool you can make is a caulking wheel. You can buy these, but a dressmaker's pattern cutter is cheaper and very nearly as good, once you've ground off the sharp edge.

The third tool you will have to buy—a small caulking iron to set wicking in places that the wheel can't handle.

Rolling in wicking needs little explanation—you get one end started and keep going, using firm but not extreme pressure. Watch for slack (oversize) seams, where it is easy to drive the wicking clear through to the inside of the planking, which you don't want to do. If you come to a slack seam, bunch the cotton wicking up to give it more thickness.

At the hood ends of the planks, don't cut off your cotton wicking; take it right around. Lay it in the rabbet seam around the plank end, and on into the next seam a little way so that a continuous strand is maintained. Then cut it off and start over again at the head of that hood end with another strand or two, making a slight overlap.

When the seams are caulked, paint right over the wicking with one coat of thinned-out flat white paint, and let it dry before you putty the seams.

While you're waiting for that paint to dry, you might ponder the antiquity of the guild of which you've just become a member. You've heard the saying, "There'll be the devil to pay." In its entirety, it runs "The devil to pay—and no pitch hot," and it goes back at least a couple of hundred years and comes straight from a shipyard. It has nothing to do with paying money to Satan. "Paying" was the old word for caulking. Furthermore, the devil wasn't even Satan. It was the seam between the keel and the garboard strake, which the old caulkers hated to pay. So, with no pitch hot, you had the equivalent of being up the well-known creek without a paddle. This same seam is also the "Devil" in "Between the Devil and the deep blue sea." In other words, you're overboard and already below the ship's hull, well started on your way to Davy Jones's Locker. These sayings seem to point to one conclusion: anything to do with boats and venturing out in them is potentially very unpleasant. You might remember this when you take your boat away from shore and out over that deep blue sea.

You can buy various seam compounds, some of them conveniently stored in tubes so you can squeeze out a ribbon, like toothpaste. They also come in cans that fit into caulking guns, like oversized cartridges, so that a press on the trigger exudes a thin line of putty. I make my own compound, so I can control the consistency of the mixture.

To make seam compound, use whiting (a powder sold under that name), boiled linseed oil, and white lead. Dump a couple of handfuls of whiting onto a pie plate, add a chunk of white lead the size of a golf ball and a slug of linseed oil. Stir the mixture until it is consistently gooey. Add more whiting for a little more stiffness, and you have your seam compound.

If you're making putty to cover nail heads set below the surface, add still more whiting until you can pick up the mixture and knead it like dough—until it feels like "boughten" putty, in other words. Press the putty over the nailhead with your thumb, and slice it clean off with a putty knife so that it covers only the nail head and not the surrounding wood.

Seam putty should be thinner than the nail head mixture, but it shouldn't be mixed to the consistency of soup; you don't want to pour it, you want it to have some body and resistance. Put the compound on a pallette and putty-knife it into the seams. Start anywhere, but as you move along keep pulling toward where you started to make sure you've filled the seam. When the compound starts surging back out of the seam, move along ahead. You don't want voids or airspaces in your puttied seams; you want them filled. Yet, as with the nailheads, you don't want the putty to be plastered onto adjoining planking, or bulging at the seams (was that phrase born in a shipyard, too?).

With the seams and nailheads all puttied, you can, if you wish, give the whole hull a coat of flat white paint.

USING the CAULKING WHEEL

Rolling wicking.

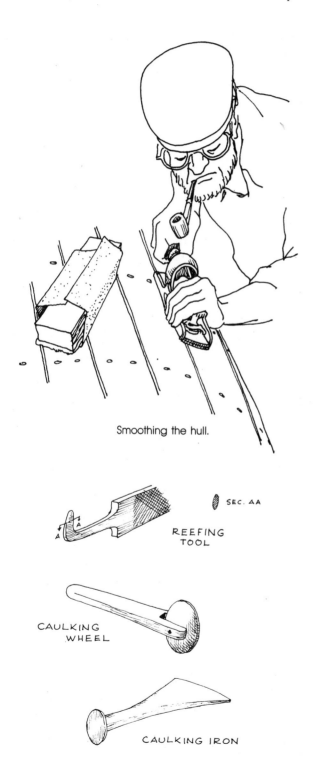

Smoothing the hull.

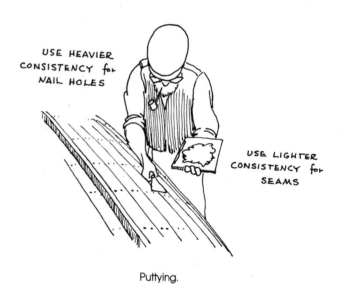

USE HEAVIER CONSISTENCY for NAIL HOLES

USE LIGHTER CONSISTENCY for SEAMS

Puttying.

SEC. AA

REEFING TOOL

CAULKING WHEEL

CAULKING IRON

Caulking tools.

12 Striking the Waterline

Striking the waterline is another one of those bugaboos in the boat-building process that needn't be difficult, for there is a simple way to do it.

Set the boat upright on a couple of sawhorses, and level it very carefully athwartships. The hull does not have to be level fore and aft. Cut a stiff stick, one and a half by three-quarter inches or so, and tack it across the transom at the height you have determined for the waterline. The stick should extend beyond the hull by a foot on each side. Now tack the center of an identical stick firmly to the stem, again at your predetermined waterline height, and make sure it is level. Brace both sticks to the floor of your shop so they can't move. Next, stretch a string, with an awl at each end by which you can anchor it, over the tops of the two horizontal sticks so that it just touches the hull amidships, at about the point of greatest beam. Tighten the string by taking a couple of turns around the stick at either the bow or the stern and secure it there with one of your awls. Repeat the process at the other end, and then drive a thumbtack snugly under the string where it touches the hull amidships. Then working from either the bow or the stern, draw the string in against the hull a little at a time, inserting more thumbtacks as the line of contact with the hull lengthens. Don't pull the string so tight that it slips down the side of the hull—it must stay straight. Now repeat the process from the midpoint of the string to its other end.

At this stage, stand off and check the string, eyeballing it dead level with its height above the floor and looking at it broad on, to spot any dips or humps. Then view it looking upward, from below. From that vantage point your waterline should show a fine curve along the length of the boat. Is the line okay? If so, put pencil marks—little dots—directly under the string at three- or four-inch intervals. Remove the string and the thumbtacks and connect all the dots, using a short stick or a light batten, depending on whether you're working alone or with a helper, and you've got it.

You may prefer a slightly sheered or rockered waterline; this is purely a matter of taste. However, the curve must be moderate and gradual. To achieve this effect, pull the string down a half-inch midships, or whatever distance your eye tells you to pull it down, and place a thumbtack over the top of the string. Then proceed as before.

There are other ways of striking a waterline. You can leave your line clear of the hull and put a carpenter's level under it with one end of the level touching the hull, at every interval where you wish to pencil in a dot; but this is rather a slow process. Or you can use a transit. But quite apart from the expense of buying a transit, why bother to do it this way?

When you've drawn your waterline, mark it off with tape, lay on a couple of coats of copper bottom paint from there down to the keel, and you're done.

You will probably feel a little timid about making the waterline your first time around, as I was, but with a little practice you'll gain confidence. You can get away with a lot, using this method, after you get over your timidity.

One day one of my in-laws, Carroll Rackliff, asked me if I would reestablish the waterline on his thirty-four-foot lobster boat. The original line had dropped out of sight forward when he changed the power plant in the boat. When I looked her over, she was resting on a lobster crate on one side. I nailed a stick across her transom at her old waterline, nailed another across her bow three inches above the old line, and simply "sighted level" between the two sticks. We struck the new line, painted it in, and duplicated it on the other side, and when she was refloated she was right on the money.

Moral: Don't be afraid to trust your eyes.

Before you paint your boat, put some scuff protection on her forward keel and stem. Use five-eighths-inch half-oval brass—a piece long enough to reach from the stem head and aft along the keel for about three feet. That will take care of all the beaching you're apt to do. Bury the after end of the brass strip in the keel so that it won't catch when you're backing off the shore.

If you're going to use the boat for working, a piece of split aluminum electrical conduit fastened along her gunwale will give protection when you're hauling gear over the side. The aluminum saws easily with a bandsaw.

Now give your boat another two coats of paint on the topsides, then paint her inside, and put her over. She's finished.

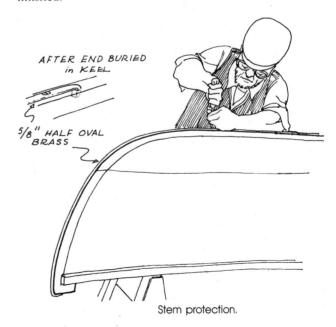

AFTER END BURIED in KEEL

5/8" HALF OVAL BRASS

Stem protection.

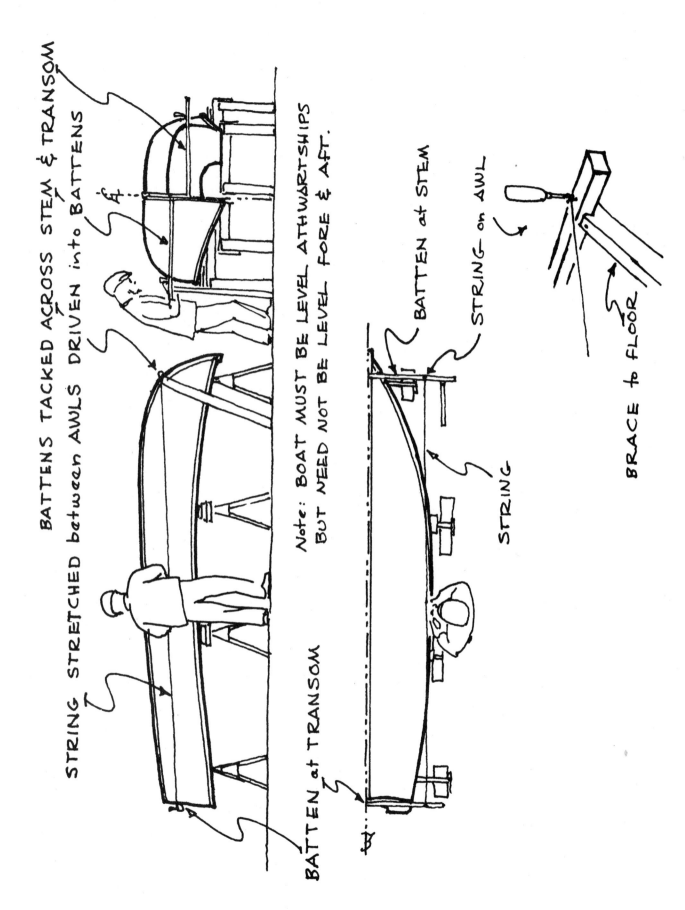

BATTENS TACKED ACROSS STEM & TRANSOM

STRING STRETCHED between AWLS DRIVEN into BATTENS

Note: BOAT MUST BE LEVEL ATHWARTSHIPS BUT NEED NOT BE LEVEL FORE & AFT.

BATTEN at TRANSOM

BATTEN at STEM

STRING on AWL

BRACE to FLOOR

STRING

Striking the waterline.

PART TWO

THE PLEASURES AND PERILS OF PLYWOOD

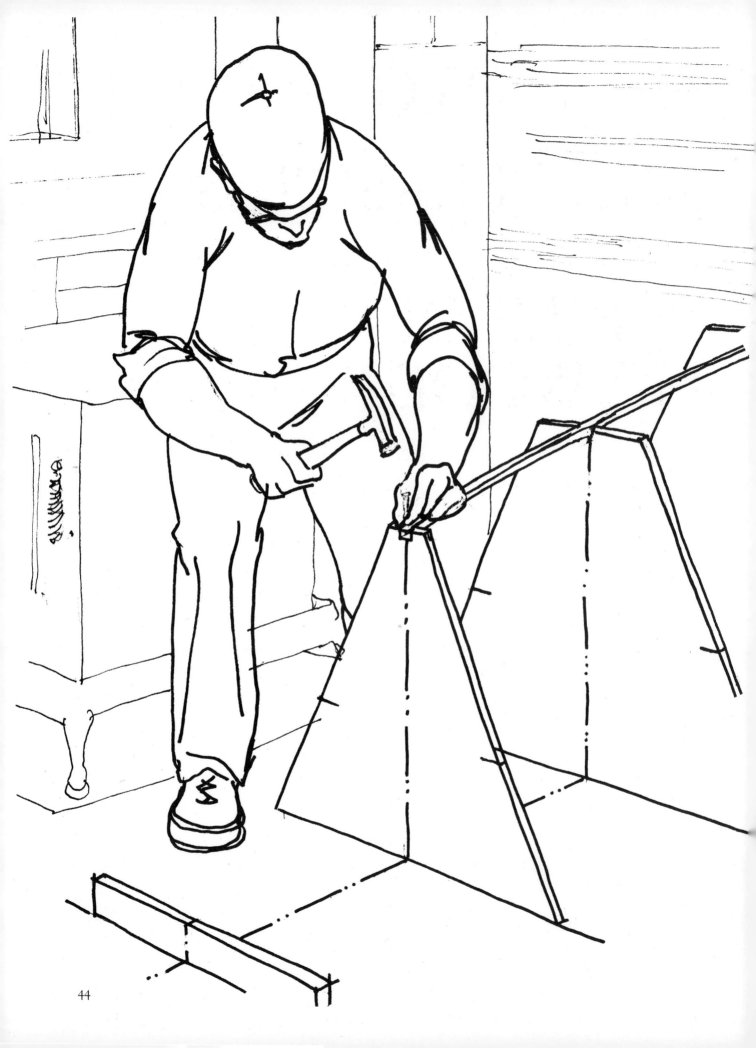

As a readily available building material, plywood is seductive, particularly to the eye of the beginner boat designer/builder. But beneath the attractive surface of this strong and durable cross-grained laminate, there lurks a hidden pitfall.

It is easy to design a pleasing shape that appears perfectly suitable for building in plywood. But when you try to assemble your neatly sawed-out components, they may simply refuse to go together at all. For a piece of plywood will obligingly bend in any one plane, but never in two.

To illustrate why I like to build in plywood, and to explain the limitations it imposes, I have chosen two existing designs and have given detailed instructions for building them. They are both from the board of naval architect Phil Bolger, and with good reason: this renowned master of innovative design has a special fondness for the small boat, and he can stretch the application of plywood to the limit of its uses. One of the Bolger designs I'm presenting here is a classic light rowing dory; the other is the only craft I have ever come across that has proved equally able under power, sail, and oar.

I've thrown in, gratis, the Payson rough-and-ready method of cloning an existing hull in fiberglass.

13 Why I Took Up with Plywood

You might call this chapter "Reflections of an Unemployed Boat-Builder."

There is no question that planking cedar on oak frames is the most enjoyable boat-building method I know. Nothing has ever given me greater satisfaction than starting with the idea for a boat and carrying right through with it, building in the traditional way. Once a beginner builder meets and conquers the challenge of plank-on-frame construction, and the anxieties that go with it, the sense of achievement is overwhelming. I felt that with my new-found skills I would be happy to go on forever planking up round-bottom boats. However, the reality of the marketplace caught up with me, and the name of that reality was fiberglass. With fiberglass, what took me a month to do in wood could be done in one day, given a mold to work with.

I couldn't lick glass builders, and I didn't really want to join them. I was in no hurry to give up sweet-smelling cedar shavings for fiberglass goop and the dust that goes with it. So I went to work turning out flat-bottom skiffs, marking time until I could figure out a way to compete successfully with fiberglass boats.

In a moment of weakness—having to do with responsibility for my financial security—I applied for a job at a brand-new and very impressive looking plant erected solely for the purpose of fiberglass-boat production. I did this even though I had, in the course of frequent visits to the plant, observed the lay-up process, the smoothing off, and the joinery work, and had had an opportunity to watch the workers come reeling out of the molds reeking of resin, their clothes coated with a cat's-hair layer of matting. In the sunlight—what little sunlight was allowed to enter the big steel building—I could see the glitter of fiberglass particles filling the air.

But luck was with me: the plant folded even before it had fairly started. The closing was very dramatic. In the middle of the night—after many thousands of dollars had been poured into the project by the state and federal governments, some of the owners, and quite a few local optimists—the head of the company loaded up his molds and what tools he could, and made for the Canadian border. He has not been seen in the area since. So they took down the big sign that said, over L.B.J.'s signature, "Better Jobs for More People," and I slammed my shop door on the kind of security you get by looking to someone else. If it was a helping hand I was looking for, I was better off looking no farther than the end of my arm.

Clearly, if you're going to go broke, whether on a big or small scale, you're better off doing it on your own in a way you enjoy.

About the same time the glass-boat plant folded, plywood was making a comeback in the marine field. A good marine grade had been developed, one with enough plies stuck together with good marine glue so that the sheet didn't delaminate in the water. The only problem with the wood was that it had a tendency to scuff when the chine of the boat ran up against the rocky teeth of the Maine coast. I had built plywood boats before, and had given it up because plywood splintered and chewed up too easily along its corners.

What began to make sense to me was to build with the new marine plywood and reinforce it with fiberglass where it was most vulnerable to scraping and banging. No, you can't get a nice round-bottom hull with all its lovely curves out of sheet of plywood, because as I mentioned in the introduction to this section plywood can't bend in two different planes at once. But plywood construction is much faster than plank-on-frame construction, and with fiberglass reinforcement it can provide virtually one-piece watertight integrity, with an average life span of twenty years or more.

So, finally making up my mind about the direction to take, I put my hollowing planes, caulking wheel, and ribband stock to one side and tucked my round-bottom molds overhead on the rafters of my shop, where they have gathered dust for a couple of decades.

With some regret? Sure. But I have found new sources of satisfaction. It takes skill to get a sixteen-foot length of plywood for the side of a boat such as the Gloucester light dory, which has some twist in it, to fit snugly and come out with a graceful sheer, all in one crack. When you can do this, you don't have to apologize to anyone, including yourself.

I don't want to discourage any newcomer to boat-building from using the traditional materials and techniques; quite the opposite. But I also want to encourage the newcomer to appreciate and enjoy the advantages of plywood, if it fits his purpose, and to assure him that plywood construction has its moments of glory.

14 Dangers of Dory Design

I'm beginning my discussion of plywood construction with the dory because just about every amateur who has lived in the plywood era immediately fixes on the dory as an ideal design for plywood—it is flat-sided, or nearly so, and flat-bottomed. Simple—no sweat. For a dory, three one-quarter-inch-by-four-foot-by-eight-foot sheets of plywood should do it.

Not so. Actually it takes considerably more skill to design a graceful and *safe* hull in the dory model, and in plywood especially, than it does to design a round-bottom hull. Everything has to come together, and come together right, because with plywood you can't count on self-adjustment as you go along, as you can when you plank on frames.

One of the dangers in designing a dory is that people who fall in love with the type seem to believe that the smaller it is the safer it will be, when actually the reverse is true.

My first experience with this fallacy came when a New York designer asked me to build a twelve-foot dory for duck hunting for a client of his in California, who was helping out by supplying all the specifications. I said sure, which was the beginning of my first lesson about the designer-builder relationship, along with my first lesson in why a small boat designed dory-style doesn't work.

The fellow in California was obviously sold on the common belief that if a boat looks like a dory, it will act like one, which will automatically make it the most seaworthy boat in the world.

When my New York designer's plans arrived, they showed a boat that in profile had a dory sheer. But it also had two transoms—both of the traditional dory tombstone shape—one at the stern, where it belonged, and one at the bow, where it did not. The boat also had very high sides, with much less flare than a dory's sides have, and it had no skeg. The reason for the high sides, I was told, was to let the thwarts be placed high enough to accommodate drawers under them to hold shotgun shells, food, and any other comforts the hunter might require.

The design was the worst possible combination of misconceptions I had ever seen, but I kept my mouth shut. I decided to build the boat without offering an opinion, since I wasn't asked for one.

She was quick to build, and two weeks later I tried her out at the request of the designer. It was like riding a bicycle for the very first time. Lacking a skeg—a small triangular keel-like projection under the stern whose function is to keep a flat-bottom boat running in a straight line—she also lacked directional control, and every time she heeled the slightest bit it was obvious that she wanted to go all the way over.

I phoned the designer and told him how his duck-hunting dory had performed; he said he'd be up to see for himself, and that maybe we had better put a skeg on the boat. So we put on a full-length skeg—it would be more accurate to call it a keel—which was about six inches deep amidships, and tried her again. Her steering was slightly improved, but she rolled just as much as before, only a little slower.

We crated her up and sent her off to California. In about a week I had a letter from the owner saying that the boat had arrived in good shape, the shipping cost had been horrendous, and that he didn't dare shoot a gun while in the boat. He was man enough to accept the blame for the fact that the design he specified didn't work, and I heard no more about it. At least he didn't shoot the designer, which reportedly has happened at least once.

You would think that when a client goes about having a creation such as this one designed for himself, he would at least first look around the ready-built or ready-designed market, or better still would check out the boats he saw being used on the water to see if anything resembling his dream-boat had in fact been made. If not, it should forewarn him to expect the worst.

Close on the heels of that experience, an artist friend

of mine, despite a keenly observing eye, decided that there should be a small dory designed just for teaching kids to row. I told him that if he had a kid he wanted drowned, to go ahead and design it. My willingness to build it was another matter altogether.

He was a good friend, though, and I hated to let him down. He persuaded me to build to his design with the understanding that he would never let a child use the boat without supervision. I thought it would be wise to let him have some part in the building process, so I left the fiberglassing to him. He was one of those people who will start off any new project with a flurry of activity but who poop out with the end in sight, and he never could bring himself to finish the job.

On his death I fell heir to the unfinished boat, since no one wanted it, including me. At first I intended to cut her in half with a chainsaw, just to make sure that no one ever risked his life in her. Then I got to thinking that she might look pretty good filled with flowers. But on the other hand, I wasn't anxious to have people wondering why a brand-new boat, built by me, was being used as a flower pot. The boat hung around the yard while I wavered between the flower garden and chainsaw solutions.

One day a retired Navy commander drove into my yard, looking for a really small dory that he could use as a tender for a larger boat. I told him I had a brand-new one that wasn't worth a damn. His attitude implied that my opinion, compared with his, was absolutely worthless, so I said: "A hundred and twenty-five bucks and she's yours—on the condition that if she doesn't work out you don't bring her back."

He did bring her back a week later, but rather than asking for his money back, he left the dory as a down payment on a bigger boat.

I was just beginning to wonder how much the chainsaw would slow down when it hit the one scabby layer of fiberglass my friend had managed to put onto the hull, when Jack Vibber, a summer visitor from Connecticut, rolled in and caught me just as I was starting to find out.

"Stop! I'll give you thirty dollars for her!" he called to me as he got out of his car.

"No way. She's not fit to go in, and I'll get thirty dollars worth of pleasure out of cutting her in half."

But fifty dollars changed my mind, and with the same warning not to bring it back, I let him drive off to Connecticut with the dory. I never heard about that boat again, and I hope I never do.

THE EXCEPTION—A GOOD SMALL DORY

Good small dories can be designed and built, but the boat I'm about to describe is not just a good small dory. She is instead the best small dory I ever saw or hope to see. She is also just big enough to deliver dory performance.

My introduction to her began on a suspiciously familiar note. A Connecticut man named Eugene Swan stopped by my shop one day and asked me to build a dory for the boys' camp he ran at Belgrade Lakes, Maine. Thinking this was just one more request for an open-top coffin for boys to learn to row in, I told him flatly that I wasn't interested. I didn't even ask him what kind of a dory he had in mind.

But Eugene is a persistent cuss in a nice way, and a few days later he walked into my shop with a set of plans in his hand and said simply: "Take a look at this."

"This" was the fifteen-foot six-inch Gloucester light dory, and the designer's name in the lower righthand corner was Philip C. Bolger, of Gloucester, Massachusetts.

She was the prettiest dory I had ever seen. She was lowsided, with a graceful sheer; more important, her seats were down low where they made sense, and she was clean as a hound's tooth inside, with only the minimum number of frames to support her shape. This dory was right up my alley, plywood construction and all, and the more I studied the drawings the more I admired them. At that time I had never heard of Phil Bolger, but it was obvious that he not only knew how to design, but was also that rare bird—a designer who knew how to build.

It's great to be excited about something, and I certainly was excited when I built the first of three of the little dories for Eugene Swan. I got so carried away that

One use for a boat that wasn't designed very well. (Photo by Brooks Townes.)

Gloucester light dory with her designer, Phil Bolger, at the oars. (Photo by Harold Adams.)

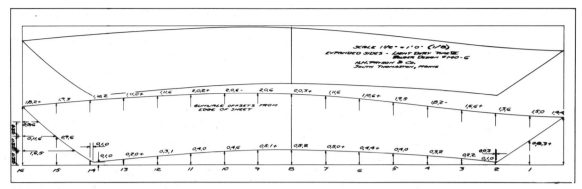

The Gloucester light dory expanded side pattern can be laid out this way as well, but using AC exterior plywood means that the builder will end up with one good side (outside) and one poor side (inside). This layout is okay for marine-grade plywood, which has two good outer surfaces.

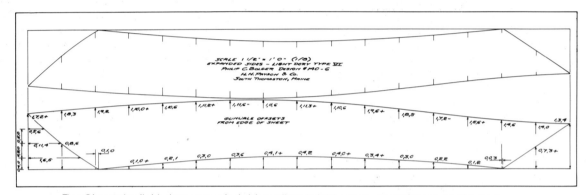

The Gloucester light dory expanded side pattern is laid out on 4×16' sheets of plywood. Flopping to a mirror image is the best way to lay the sides out.

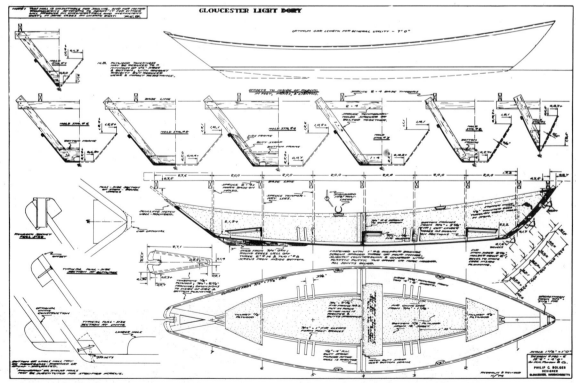

Gloucester light dory construction plan showing mold stations, building jig, and her lines in profile as well as plan view (looking down at her).

I wrote Bolger, telling him how refreshing it was to see something so totally different yet so good, and I included a photo of the first dory I completed.

I learned something about design very soon after that. Phil Bolger wrote back, congratulating me on the building job but regretting that I had taken out the little hook aft that he had designed into the boat's sheer. I had missed it, he said, by three-quarters of an inch.

I started to write back to him that I hadn't made a mistake; that I had decided she was a little low-sided, and had therefore straightened the sheer a hair from amidships to the transom. But before I mailed the letter I measured the sheer in the area he questioned, and I got quite a fright. My variation from his plans was exactly three-quarters of an inch.

Phil Bolger is a fellow you don't want to try putting anything past. I saw that he was right, that by raising and straightening the sheer I'd spoiled the looks of the boat. I put the sheer back where it was supposed to be in subsequent boats, and there it has remained in every one of the one hundred-plus Gloucester light dories I have built.

The dory had another valuable lesson for me. Like hundreds of other people, I thought that because she was so pretty she would perform as well under power and sail as under oars. When I wrote Bolger and asked him about this (showing I had learned to consult him first, anyway) he replied that he wished he had a dollar for every letter he had had suggesting this, and he explained point by point just why the dory should be rowed, and only rowed. I respected his judgment, but after working for certain unconvinced customers I had to learn this for myself.

One such customer, who claimed to have some skill in boat designing, demanded a motor well in his dory for an outboard. I couldn't persuade him otherwise, so in it went. I tried the boat out myself with a two-horse British Seagull in the relatively calm waters of Camden Harbor. Running straight, she wasn't too bad, but the instant I tried to turn her she snapped her rail right down to the water and tried to throw me out, probably in disgust.

My next stubbornly wrong-headed customer wanted a sailing version, so we stepped a standing lug rig in her, stepped well forward, and hung a rudder on her transom; there was no mention of a centerboard or leeboard. When we tried her, nothing happened, she just sat there broadside to the wind. Because the whole deal hadn't looked very promising to me, I hadn't suggested a centerboard or leeboard myself. I didn't think either one would make much of a difference, and I rather thought I could be saving a life or two just by keeping my mouth shut instead of encouraging further experimentation. Today, I say a firm *no* whenever anyone asks me to build an oddball boat, or wants me to deviate from the designer's plan for a boat like the Gloucester light dory. If the builder gives in to a customer's whims, the customer will be embarrassed when his ideas fail to work and he will get mad at the designer and the builder just

because they insisted from the start that his ideas wouldn't work. I'll agree to allow a choice of materials—up to a point—and I'll paint a boat any color the customer wants. But that's it.

If you are designing and building a boat for yourself, you have to develop a split personality in this regard, seeing yourself as both the customer and designer. As the customer, never let yourself impose your whims on you as the designer/builder. If, for example, you decide you want to design a good small rowing dory, don't. Build Phil Bolger's Gloucester light dory instead. And when you design any type of boat for yourself, don't stray too far away from the models you know have been successful. As I've already indicated, if you don't see your pet ideas floating around on the water, there's probably a reason for it.

And even if you don't want a rowing dory and aren't going to build a Gloucester light rowing dory, you can still learn a great deal about building with plywood by reading through the next chapter describing exactly how Bolger's boat should be built.

I can't let this preliminary description of the Gloucester light dory go by without giving some examples of her virtues. Gerald Greely of Gloucester set a course record for the annual rowing race around Cape Ann in one of these, covering nineteen and a half miles of open water in four hours and twenty minutes. My son Neil used one to win the first annual Camden Harbor rowing race against all comers, any size and any style. Even at my advanced age I won the same race the following year in still another of these dories, and did it despite the handicap of a thirty-pound rock concealed under an oilskin jacket in the bow, courtesy of Neil and his brother David.

I never did go looking for heavy weather in my own Gloucester, having had my share of it in other boats in the past. I trucked one of them to a customer in Belfast, Maine, on a day with a stiff northeast wind and plenty of whitecaps, expecting him to leave it on the beach that day. But he was a deep-water merchant veteran, and had to try her out. Moreover, of all directions to choose, he struck off downwind, hell bent for leather. I watched him row out a half-mile or more, wondering how he would make out when he turned around and headed back. When he did, I could see that he was gaining at every stroke, and steadily at that.

Since the Gloucester light dory is a little tender—she will heel down rather quickly with a substantial off-center weight injudiciously placed—you don't want to step aboard the first time out with both hands in your pockets. But you will soon get used to her ways and you will learn that, while she likes to roll down to her gunwale, she stops right there; she won't go on over because of the reserve buoyancy the flare of her sides gives her. She can weather a treacherous chop.

In the course of describing how to build this little boat, I'll drop a word in about tools here and there, but I'll give you my entire philosophy on tools in a later chapter.

15 Building the Gloucester Light Dory

Thirteen years ago, when I started building Gloucester light dories, it made sense to use only the best materials: marine-grade plywood, oak rails, special marine glues—the works.

Perhaps you still want the very best and hang the cost. If that's the way you feel and you're a skilled craftsman confident that you can do the job right the first time, without spoilage and waste, go right ahead. At this writing (1982), you can expect to pay about three hundred dollars for your materials, including those for the jig on which you'll build the boat.

A dozen years ago the cost was half that, or less. And you can still build the dory inexpensively, even today, but you'll have to compromise on materials. You can build a cheaper, much lighter version you yourself can car top, by going to quarter-inch AC exterior plywood, which is the grade used in house construction; you can use spruce or pine for framing instead of oak, and cut your chines and gunwales from the clearest sixteen-foot two-by-fours that you can find.

For about thirty dollars, you can buy three sheets of quarter-inch AC plywood from which to make the sides and bottom. The way the dory is laid out, you can get both sides from two eight-foot plywood sheets, butted as shown at the center thwart, and the bottom can be made from one sheet split in two and ends butted with a butt-strap right under the bottom frame amidships.

There will be some waste in using an eight-foot sheet of plywood for the bottom when one twelve-foot sheet of marine-grade plywood would do it, but three sheets of quarter-inch AC exterior grade will cost less than one twelve-foot sheet of half-inch thick marine-grade. And since the bottom is only two feet wide and will be glassed over, you needn't worry about strength unless you plan to use your dory in a crashing surf on a beach full of boulders, in which case you'd want to keep to the heavier three-eighths-inch sides and half-inch bottom.

If you ask "Why not compromise and go to three-eighths-inch exterior grade all around?"—the answer is very simple: for the last several years the quality of this heavier exterior plywood has been so poor it is hardly worth lugging home, because it has been made with extremely thin outer layers and a thick, water-absorbing core, with voids running through each sheet that make you wonder how its purveyors ever get it into their racks without having it fall apart from the strain. Strangely enough, though, the cheaper AC grade in one-quarter-inch three-ply wood with one good outer surface, a good core, and one bum outer surface is better than the higher AB grade exterior which has two very pretty surfaces and a core that would shame a crooked politician.

The core is the important element in plywood simply because you can't deal with what you can't see. I've built a number of boats with quarter-inch AC with no

failures, and since the price is right, I'll probably continue. However, before you do any building with this wood, you should fill any rough outer-surface knotholes and imperfections with a mixture of sawdust and glue, or auto-body filler, while the sheet is lying flat.

If you decide to go for broke with marine-grade plywood, pick up two three-eighths-inch-by-eight-foot sheets for the sides, and a half-inch-by-twelve-foot sheet for the bottom. If you want to avoid butt joints in the sides, get your three-eighths-inch sheets in sixteen-foot lengths.

You will also need material for the building jig, and for mold framing, if you decide to employ the jig as shown in the plans. I'll list the wood required for this construction here, and the fastenings too, but don't rush out and buy all this, as I am recommending an alternative method of setting-up that you will probably prefer.

Using the jig method, you will need eighty linear feet of spruce or pine, measuring one inch by four inches in cross section, with which to make your molds. For fastenings, these will call for one gross of one-and-one-half-inch galvanized screws. The jig itself would require two sixteen-foot two-by-fours for longitudinal supports and nine twelve-foot two-by-fours for cross members, and eighteen quarter-inch or five-sixteenths-inch black-iron carriage bolts to fasten these members together.

The alternative method does not require any mold-framing material. Using this technique you cut your molds from plywood, and tack them in place right on your shop floor. Two sheets of one-half-inch plywood or heavier of any grade will suffice.

The choice of glue is up to you—epoxy, resorcinol, or dry powder, as long as it's a marine glue. I see nothing wrong with the dry-powder type for this kind of work, and it's cheaper. The main thing in using powdered glue is to mix it to the consistency of heavy cream. Use plenty of it. When you force a joint together and glue squeezes out, you know you've used enough.

For fastenings, you'll need a pound each of one-inch, one-and-one-eighth-inch and one-and-one-quarter-inch number 13 bronze ringed nails; a box of one-and-one-quarter-inch number 10 bronze wood screws to fasten the thwarts and the Wilcox-Crittenden oarlock side plates; and a few two-inch number 14 bronze screws for the skeg.

Save yourself some time and trouble by buying a Fuller combination countersink-counterbore for the number 10 screws, a Stanley Screwmate for the number 14s, and a five-sixty-fourths drill bit to bore for the wire nails. You will certainly have to pre-bore before driving fastenings into oak. These special timesavers don't cost a great deal, and I wouldn't be without them.

As for the rest of your battery of tools, you would naturally be able to use a shopful; but I think that it's best to find out what you really need as you go along.

Why stock up a tool room when the first boat you build might also be your last? I recommend that you use what tools you have and buy only the additional tools that are really necessary. For special purposes, such as the long cuts required making gunwales and chines, take your stock to somebody who already has the tools for the job.

It would be nice to have a table saw, a hand power saw, and a bandsaw, but I would never buy any of these to build just one boat. Because I'm a commercial builder, every tool I buy is an investment in time saved. But to the one-time builder, time isn't all that important; the amateur doesn't mind spending time knocking off corners, for example—a job I'd do with my router in no time flat.

A few good chisels, a decent (not a dime-store) hammer, a 10-point handsaw (not stainless steel), a low-angle block plane, a quarter-inch electric drill, and all the clamps you can afford or borrow add up to a good start. Add a bit-brace and screwdriver bits for number 10 and number 14 screws—it's nearly impossible to drive screws into oak by hand, even when they've been soaped—and that's it for starters.

Now—since one hour of planning is worth two hours of work—plop yourself down in your favorite chair and study your plans. Build the Gloucester light dory in your head before you touch steel to wood. Note that the plans are drawn to the scale of one and one-half inch equals one foot. Also take note that the measurements given are expressed in terms of feet, inches, and eighths of an inch, with a plus sign after the last figure to indicate another sixteenth of an inch. This is universal for all boat plans, including those for an aircraft carrier (unless the Navy has gone metric). Use your scale rule. Any time you wonder about a dimension between the little arrows, check it out with the scale rule. If you find an indispensable dimension that hasn't been specified, lay your rule on it and see what it should be.

As with all boat plans, those for the light dory establish a baseline and a centerline, from which all heights and widths are measured. Study the jig set-up profile: the baseline of the boat lies on top of the two-by-four jig support longitudinals. If you are going to use the jig method, once you've built the jig, your first order of business is to draw patterns from which to make molds for each station on the plan. The jig itself is an upside down set of molds, stiff enough to permit bending the dory's sides and bottom over them. If you decide in favor of the alternative method, your molds will be set up directly on the floor of your shop, and the floor is your baseline. Either way, you will be building the dory upside down.

There is more than one way to build any boat. From my experience in building a variety of skiffs, the upside-down approach to the Gloucester light dory is the best. I like to get the biggest units or sections of a boat done first; in this case, the dory's basic shape. In a hull like this I hold up on the interior until the hull has been righted.

There is also more than one way to build a boat wrong. An amateur builder working on a Gloucester once called me to report that he was having trouble fit-

ting the chines. I listened for fifteen minutes before I grasped the incredible truth: that instead of fitting the chines in place after the sides were on, he had fastened the chines to the stem and transom first, and was now trying to fit the sides and the bottom to fill out this fragile skeleton.

DEVELOPING THE MOLDS

You can lay out your mold sections in two ways—by the hands-and-knees method on the floor, or working while standing upright, using a sheet of five-eighths-inch plywood set up on saw horses for a drafting table. This plywood platform need be only big enough to accommodate the full-size drawing of the largest mold, but the standard four-foot-by-eight-foot plywood sheet will give you the advantage of greater steadiness, as well as easier manipulation of your drafting tools. I recommend the latter method, which relieves you of the chore of crawling around on the floor. So let's begin by drawing in the seven mold stations on the sheet of plywood.

Nail an eight-foot two-by-four, or a board with straight edges, along one of the long edges of the plywood sheet, and call its inboard edge the baseline. From the center of this two-by-four or board, erect a line perpendicular to it. This will be your centerline.

Let's start with the mold shape for station number 4—the largest one. Butt your rule against the baseline and measure up along the centerline the distance between the bottom of that section and the baseline, which the plan indicates is 2—5—4+. Remember, the first number always represents feet, the second inches, and the third eighths of inches. So we have two feet, five inches, and a half-inch, to which we add a sixteenth because of the plus sign. Expressed in conventional terms, the distance is two feet, five and nine-sixteenths inches. Mark the centerline at that point. Now measure off the half-width of the bottom of station number 4, which the plan shows as 0—11—7, and translates to eleven and seven-eighths inches. Put a square on the

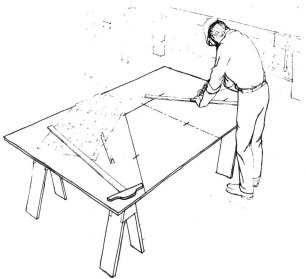

On the Gloucester light dory, laying off molds on a sheet of plywood.

centerline where you've just marked it, and project a line of that length at right angles to the centerline.

The distance of the sheerline from the baseline is shown as 1—2—6, or one foot, two and three-quarters inches. Mark this on the centerline, measuring from the baseline, and square off from that point the indicated half-width at the sheer of 1—11—5+ (one foot, eleven and eleven-sixteenths inches). Draw a straight line linking these two half-width points and extending down to the baseline. You now have the side flare of the dory at its widest cross-section. Duplicate these lines on the other side of the center-line, and you have the full-size mold outline at station number 4.

Now you can lay the spruce framing material you are using for molds right on the penciled drawing, mark and cut and fasten them together, using three of your inch-and-a-half galvanized screws at each joint; screws hold better than nails, and you avoid the bounce you get when hammering nails.

You can save time by using the same baseline-center-line set-up for drawing all the mold sections, using the

same space with different colored pencils to eliminate confusion.

If you have difficulty locating the three-figure dimensions needed to lay out the remaining six station molds, examine the sectional drawing of mold station number 4. You will see where the distances used in the example just discussed are located; they are so placed in each of the mold stations shown in the plan.

ERECTING THE MOLDS

The next step, if you are using the jig set-up to build your dory, is to erect your molds on the longitudinal two-by-fours that serve as the foundation of the jig. Mark off the mold locations on the longitudinals, as shown in profile. To fasten the molds to these two-by-fours, use quarter-inch or five-sixteenths-inch carriage bolts, recessing their heads. When the molds are plumb and square, lock them together with a longitudinal board spanning all seven, fastened to the molds with nails. Add diagonal bracing to your jig, and the job is done.

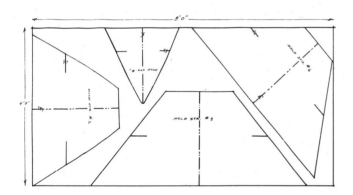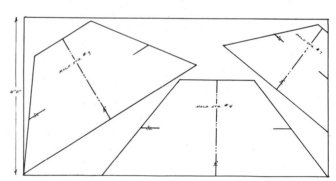

Plywood molds, from two pieces of half-inch 4 × 8′ ply. This is diagrammatic only—station dimensions should be lifted from plans. Also, remember to mark your centerline and sheer line.

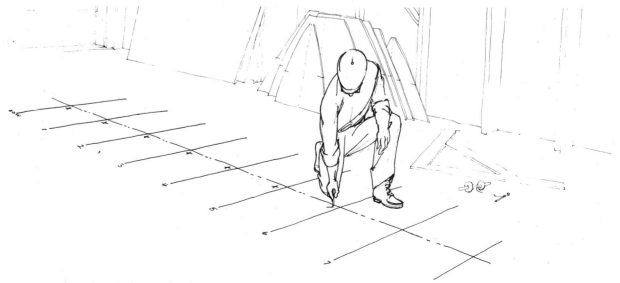

The centerline and station locations of the Gloucester light dory.

Author checks end fit of the dory's sides.

I grant that this is a lot of work to get through before you really start building your boat. So if time is important to you, and you'll use your jig for only one or two boats, choose the faster method of erecting molds cut from plywood and set directly on the floor. This jig is flimsy compared to the one described above. It requires careful checking and must be set up on a good flat surface. Yet it does save time, and it is cheaper.

With careful placement, you can cut all seven molds from two four-foot-by-eight-foot plywood sheets.

Whichever way you choose, be sure the jig is aligned to each of the mold centerlines, and fasten it securely to the floor so that it won't move or wiggle when you spring the dory's sides around the molds.

STEM AND TRANSOM

The next two items on the agenda are the stem and the transom, which must be carefully aligned with their centerlines matching the centerlines of the molds in order to get the true shape of the sides.

Make the tombstone transom to the dimensions shown, from half-inch marine plywood, and frame it with three-quarter-inch-by-two-and-a-half-inch pieces of oak. Don't try to cut the exact shape of the top of the transom, with its sculling notch and curvature; instead, leave a couple of inches at the top and cut if off square (don't forget that the framing must be left long enough to extend down onto the cross-tie of the jig, or the floor). The transom top can be shaped later. Both the outboard edge of the transom and its frame must be sawed to a forty-two-and-a-half-degree bevel and then assembled.

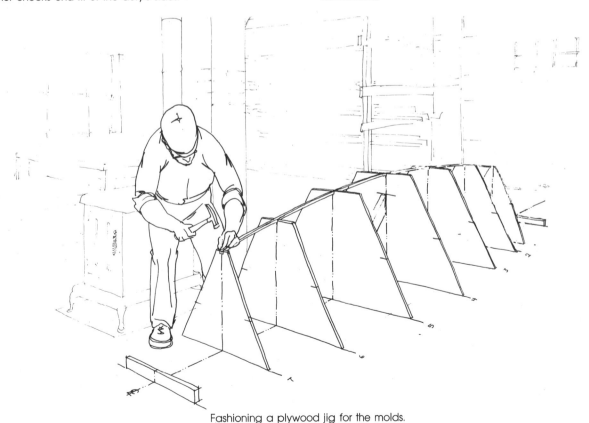

Fashioning a plywood jig for the molds.

The transsom is cut to dimensions and beveled to forty-two and a half degrees as shown.

The outboard edges of the transom frames are cut at a forty-two and a half degrees, but the straight cut is more easily made on a table saw.

The transom-frame stock is cut long enough to provide two frames with some extra, and is then clamped so that the transom and frame edges match flush.

The second frame is positioned so the bevels match, and a long mitre line is marked and cut where the two converge on the bottom of the transom.

After the transom frames are glued and nailed, the filler for the sculling notch is marked and cut to fit in place on the transom.

Setting the transom in place on the jig is a matter of getting it centered, plumb, and at the proper height, and then nailing it in place.

54

The stem is oak, sided (that is, having a thickness) two and a half inches, and molded (having a profile) about two inches. Again, don't try to cut the stem exactly to length, but make the bottom (in upside-down terms) continuing along the stem curve. There is no point in being accurate when accuracy isn't needed at this stage, for while the designer's plan shows every dimension as being precise right down to the pencil mark, that accuracy doesn't usually exist in the real boat. In fact, exactness is rarely achieved by the builder, whether amateur or professional. It is much easier to take a little off later than to add a little on; and it is good insurance to leave a little leeway.

Using your bandsaw, cut the oak stem to the profile shown in the plan, and mark a centerline on each face, all around—both fore and aft. Now cut the stem bevel by setting your bandsaw at thirty degrees. This will mean undercutting the bevel a little, but it leaves the centerline on the face of the stem by a safe margin; the stem can then be worked down by hand.

In order to clamp the stem in your vise with one side up and shape that side down to the line, take a piece of the bevel strip you sawed and nail it right back on the stem again temporarily, using small nails. Repeat this process for the other side of the stem when you're ready to shape it. What you are doing is giving the vise some wood to grip without marring the stem itself.

Now erect your stem and transom in place, and mark the chine and the sheer on both. You can now establish the shape of the plywood sides. It is good practice because this method of taking off the side shape is another form of spiling and is used again when building the Thomaston Galley.

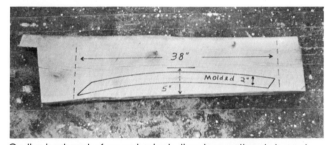

On the best part of an oak plank, the stem pattern is traced.

After rough cutting the oak to a manageable size, the stem is cut to shape on the bandsaw.

Clamped in the vise, the stem is planed smooth. A spokeshave works well for the inside curve.

As the smoothing progresses, use the trisquare to be certain that the fore and aft faces are square to the sides.

When the smoothing is complete, use the trisquare to strike centerlines on the fore and aft faces of the stem.

The stem bevel of thirty degrees is rough cut on the bandsaw leaving enough wood to smooth up to the lines by hand.

THE SIDES

Begin by cutting two battens from one-inch-by-half-inch pine or any other wood that will bend with a true curve, and tack them along the molds at the chine and sheer marks.

Next, take a sheet of construction building paper—the orange kind sold under that name at building-supply firms and some hardware stores and lumber yards—and staple it right onto the battens and the stem and transom edges, smoothing out all the wrinkles as you fasten it down. Mark the outline of the side all around, remove the paper, and trim it to the lines you have marked. This is your pattern for the two sides of your dory.

I don't think it's worth the work to cut half of each side from an eight-foot sheet of plywood and then butt the halves together. Instead, I strongly recommend using a sixteen-foot sheet of plywood and cutting each side out in one piece. So far, I know of no one who has ever built one of these dories with butted side-panels.

If you do use butted sides, begin by laying your pattern on the two eight-foot sheets that you have first butted together, being careful to shift the pattern around so as to be able to get both sides from the two sheets. Trace the outlines of the sides, leaving a half-inch or so clearance around the tracing of the pattern. Now cut out the sides and fasten a temporary plywood butt-strap to hold the two halves of the side together on the outside of the butt joint, so that this additional thickness of wood won't fall afoul of the chine and sheer battens when you spring the side around them again for the final trial fit.

In the final butting, put the straps on the inside of each pair of panels, cutting them to fall short of the

When both sides have been beveled, the waste is saved intact, to be temporarily fastened back in place.

A few small nails will suffice to tack each waste piece back to the stem.

With one waste piece tacked on, the stem can be clamped in the vise to be planed to the lines.

Set the stem in place on the jig, being sure that it is centered, plumb and at the right height. Nail it in place top and bottom from the aft side.

The side pattern is laid out (mirror image) on two sheets of four-by-eight plywood. Buttstraps are nailed before sides are cut.

Bent around the molds and clamped in place, the unusual shape of the side suddenly makes sense. The bevel on the stemhead support allows clamp pressure without slippage.

chines so that there will be room for the chines when you install them later from the inside. Be sure to keep your right and left sides firmly in mind when you make these butt joints. You must also cut away the butt-strap thickness from mold number 4 where the straps will fall. Fasten the butt-straps with flat-headed smooth-wire number 14 copper nails and clench their points, turning them back into the wood.

(Phil Bolger's notes say that you should install the butt-straps after the hull is righted, but he must have had an entirely different technique in mind—one that to this day I have never been able to figure out.)

If you wish, you can skip the pattern method for making the sides entirely, whether you're using eight- or sixteen-foot sheets, but I don't advise it. If you're using the full-length sheet, you can simply saw it in two lengthwise, bend the half-sheet around the battens, and mark directly on it; but it will be more awkward to handle and fit. If you do it this way, be sure you leave a half-inch overhang on the transom end of the side for the time being.

When you have cut out the corners of your molds to allow for installing the chines, you can nail the sides of the boat to the tombstone and the stem. Phil Bolger offers the skimpily skilled builder the alternative of installing outside chines rather than inside chines. If you choose to go this way, you don't have to notch out your mold corners. However, inside chines make for a much handsomer boat. Besides, I've found that I can get two bottoms out of one twelve-foot plywood sheet by adding just a sliver of plywood at the edge amidships, and the inside chines will be right there to back up this little joint.

Begin putting on the sides by bending one of them around and tacking it temporarily at the stem and the transom. You will need clamps to pull the bow end down snugly against the stem, and for this the Jorgensen C-clamps are just right. This C-clamp has a V-notch on the clamp pad that fits right onto the stem and won't slip off while you're applying pressure. It's the only clamp I've seen that's made that way, and I've found it so useful in so many applications that I think Jorgensen would be well-advised to tout its utility in their ads.

Are you certain that the sides lie and fit just as they should? Then loosen the clamps at the bow, slather the stem with glue, and clamp the side back in place. Pre-bore for the bronze one-and-one-eighth-inch ringed nails, drilling a staggered pattern; then drive the nails home into the stem and set the heads slightly with a quarter-inch machinist's punch.

Before you drill for the fastenings at the transom end of the side panel, sight across the transom and, with a straight-edge, draw a line half the thickness of the framing away from the edge of the transom, right down the side panel. At this location the angle between the transom and the side is such that, without this line as a guide, it is all too easy to drive a nail out through the transom framing face. Pre-bore for the fastenings staggered along a line parallel to the after face of the transom, then repeat the gluing and fastening of the sides in the same manner as for the stem.

Whenever you're using glue, keep a bucket of warm water handy, and use a rag to wipe off excess glue just as soon as it appears.

If you install your chines outside, nail them from the inside of the hull. But take it from me, it's good boat-building experience to install the chines on the inside; it's good for the ego, too, to see how skillful you are at wrapping them in there, with the proper bevel and end fit.

When you look at the side panels laid out flat on the floor, they look nothing at all like they do when they're in place on your boat. The curve of the chines is just as illusory. The chines will go in much more easily if they're shaped to follow the curve of the bottom of the dory—but just what is that curve? If you try to reproduce the bottom curve only as it looks in profile, the chines won't slip in peacefully because there are actually two curves—the curve of the bottom and the curve of the sides where they meet the bottom. The chine won't match these curves in the fitting process even though your eye tells you that they will. The proper curve of the chine should be as close as possible to the curve of the chine of the side panel when it is laid out flat on the floor.

When you saw out the chines, use the natural springing tendency of the wood to your advantage. If you can cut the chines from a live-edged piece of oak, so much the better. Note the natural curve of the tree, and approximate that in making your cut. Set your hand power saw to a thirty-eight-degree angle, and saw along the curved line you've drawn on your oak stock with a batten. Leaving your saw at the same angle, set the rip guard to the width of the chines and saw out two chines

The side is glued to the stem and fastened with one-and-one-eighth-inch anchorfast nails into prebored holes. Set the heads below flush with a nail set.

After marking out the thickness of transom and frame on the side, the glue is spread and the side fastened in place.

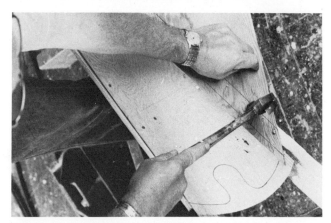

Lines drawn on the side show the builder the limits of nailing the side to the transom frame without hitting thin air. (Photo by Bill Robelen 4th.)

in succession. This will ensure that the bevel will be the same on both edges of the two chines you have just cut, and will avoid a top edge that is square against the hull and will form a water pocket.

The thirty-eight degree setting is just right in the stern area for bottom fit, and will obviate much trimming of

A simple jig holds the chine for sanding.

The other side is fastened in the same way and guided into place by leveling with the first side.

the chines there to make the bottom lie flat across; however, the flare of the sides changes about ten degrees in the forward section, and there the inboard edges of the chines will be a little too high. They will have to be flattened slightly with a plane to let the bottom make wood-to-wood contact flat across.

The next step is to spring the chines in and cut them to make a butt-fit against both the stem and the transom. The notches in the molds to receive the chines should be cut sufficiently open to leave a little room for juggling, as the forward ends must be slipped down the stem, then pulled in to the sides and the chines must be slid aft through the notches to butt up against the tombstone framing.

In order to get the correct end shapes for your chine, make two patterns, using pieces of chine about one foot long, and cut one to fit the stem and the other to fit the transom. Clamp the chine itself down on a couple of sawhorses, and—keeping in mind the helpful curve of the wood, so that you make your shaping cuts on the correct side of the chine—shape its forward end to match the stem pattern.

The next step is to determine the correct length of the chine before you shape its transom end. You can get it right to a cat's whisker. Open up your folding six-foot rule, butt it up against the stem and, with the rule held close against the side, follow the curve the chine will have to take and make a mark at six feet back from the stem. Lay off the same distance on the chine, again keeping in mind just how the forward bevel meets the stem. Next, butt the rule against the tombstone framing, following the curve the chine will make (you will have to fold up a couple of joints of the rule to do this) and bring the extension end out to touch the original six-foot mark. Apply this measurement to the chine at its six-foot mark and you have the length the chine will have to have to fit against both stem and transom. Duplicate the bevel of your stern pattern stick on the after end of the chine, and you'll have an exact fit in length and end shapes with this chine, or one that is as close as is humanly possible.

Now spring the chine into position, dry, aligning the two six-foot marks—the one on the chine and the one on the side panel of the boat—and clamp it, working from the middle toward the ends. You'll find that you will need an extra clamp to pull the chine up to the edge of the side of the boat. Hook the clamp under the chine, rest the screw pad on the side, and screw the chine into position.

If the chine is a little long, take a half-worn-out saw whose blade has worked down to a skinny point and use it to trim the troublesome end, holding the blade flat against either the transom frame or the stem. Then fit the second chine.

Take the chines out, apply glue lavishly, and clamp them back in place; then fasten them with one-inch bronze nails, spaced three to four inches apart. Pre-bore for these and drive them from the outside.

If you have fitted in the chines so they don't need even a smidgin of putty, congratulate yourself and treat yourself to a beer.

An accurate fit at the chines is obtained by scribing the compound bevel on a short pattern, then transferring the cut to the actual chine.

Chine fitted to the stem.

The inside chine used by the author is laid out by means of his six-inch folding rule, the corner of which butts up against the stem.

The length and six-inch location marks are then laid out on each chine.

When the exact length has been determined for the chines and the compound bevel marked on the ends, they can be cut with the circular saw set at thirty-three degrees for the stem and thirty-eight degrees for the transom.

Fit the chines dry first (no glue). Aligning the six-inch reference marks exactly, you can clamp the chine in place at the center and check the fit at the ends. If it is slightly off, or long, it can be helped by running a sharp saw between the end and the stem or transom.

When all is well, spread the glue on the chine, let it set for a few minutes, and install it once more.

PUTTING ON THE BOTTOM

The next step is to cut off the bottoms of the stem and the transom flush with the chines and, using a straight-edge as a guide, mow everything down absolutely flat with a plane, so that the bottom will have a proper bearing. Before you put the bottom on, cut some small softwood wedges and slip them into the notches between the chines and the jig molds, tacking them lightly to the chines with brads. These wedges will keep the sides from pulling in while you are driving nails through the bottom into the chines.

There is nothing to fitting the bottom. Lay the bottom plywood sheet on the hull, tack it at each end, and mark around the sides of the boat. Then take the sheet off, and with your hand power saw set at thirty degrees, saw right to the line. Use a planer blade that is set just deep enough to barely cut through the plywood, and the curve of your cut won't be too much for your saw. The thirty-degree bevel reduces the amount of wood you'll have to remove from the edges of the sawed-out bottom by hand and improves your chances of nailing it down without coming through the inboard face of the chines, because you will be able to see what you're doing.

Put plenty of glue on the chines and set the bottom down in place. Check for good fit all around and tack the bottom down at each end so it can't move. Starting at the middle, pre-bore for the inch-and-a-quarter bronze ringed nails. Keep the drill at an angle to match the flare of the sides and bore the holes slightly staggered, about three inches apart.

Don't be bashful about driving the nails home, and set them good and hard. Round off the corners of the bottom edge, including the stem and transom frames. Now free the stem and set your boat—for now she IS a boat—right-side up on sawhorses. If you built her on a jig, you're through with that now, so move it outside the shop.

Clamp it firmly in place, pre-bore, and fasten into it with one-inch anchorfast nails. Check for excess glue and wipe it away with a damp cloth.

Cut off the excess length of the stem and transom on the bottom, as well as the excess at the ends of the sides.

Plane down the remainder so that the joints are smooth and flush.

Plane the bottom edges of the sides flat and level with the chines so that the bottom will lie perfectly flat upon them.

61

To prevent any tendency of the sides to creep inward due to the angle of the nails from the bottom, tack some small wedges between mold and chine wherever there are gaps.

Strike a centerline on the bottom sheet and place it so it lines up precisely with the centerlines of stem and transom. The curve of the sides is then traced on the sheet.

Remove the flip the bottom sheet, and cut the marked curve at a thirty-degree bevel. If you're using a half-sheet there will be a pair of short, straight-edged lengths amidships, along which slivers will be glued.

After spreading glue upon the chines, with some help tack the bottom in place on the stem and transom centerlines.

Pre-bore for the one-and-a-quarter-inch anchorfast nails into the chines, following the angle of the sides.

Drive the nails from amidships out to the ends, but do not try to drive them flush or you risk breaking their heads. Set them all later with a quarter-inch machinists punch.

Glue and tack the amidships sliver in place.

FINISHING THE HULL

All you've got left to do is the gunwales and the interior work; that's except for the skeg, which has to wait until the bottom has been fiberglassed.

When the boat is no longer braced by the jig or the plywood molds, you'll find that the sides will have pulled in about three-quarters of an inch. To spread the sides properly, cut a stick to the exact inside beam at mold number 4, and tack it from side to side at the gunwales. Leave this "spreader" stick in place until the interior work has been completed.

Next, draw a centerline along the entire length of the bottom, mark off the seat locations as they are indicated on the plan, and square off the transverse lines for them. Each of the three seats—bow, amidships, and stern—rests on a seat frame and on risers running fore and aft along the sides. Each seat frame is made of three-quarter-inch oak, and is five and one-half inches deep; you can take their shape from the plans or from your molds, as each one falls on a station. Seat risers are made from leftover chine material, and the seats themselves are half-inch plywood, strengthened along the underside of their forward edges with a strip of three-quarter-inch-by-one-and-a-half-inch oak, set back far enough not to interfere with the seat frames.

The midships seat frame goes in square, with no bevel anywhere. Fit it to the sides and bottom, and mark all around it. Take it out and pre-bore through the bottom from inside for your inch-and-a-quarter bronze nails, spacing the holes about three inches apart. Glue the seat frame lavishly along its bottom and edges and put it back in place; then drill up through the bottom, using the same holes, and into the seat frame (a helper's

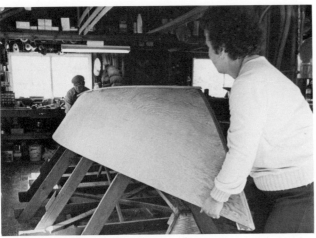

Free the boat from the jig by cutting the excess transom framing and pulling the nails you drove into the stem.

The midseat frame is fitted and marked off so that holes can be bored from the inside and fasteners anchored from the outside.

There is nothing like a finished hull to give you a feeling of great accomplishment.

The cant (side) frames are laid out on a piece of oak and cut out on the bandsaw.

63

hand comes in handy here) and drive your nails home.

The risers, which are cut short at the forward ends so as not to interfere with the oak strengthening piece across the underside of the seat, are nailed and glued, using one-inch bronze ringed nails, for which you pre-bore from the outside of the boat's side panel.

In addition to the seat frame, there are two cant frames (one on each side of the boat) made of three-quarter-by-three-inch oak. These extend from the bottom of the boat to the gunwale. They are glued and fastened with one-and-one-quarter-inch bronze nails, following the usual process of pre-boring from the outside of the hull, so that they lie just aft of the midships seat frame. They are also fastened to the seat frame, with three one-and-one-quarter-inch number 10 bronze screws. These are driven from forward, where they won't show—the seat will extend over them.

The risers for this midships seat, being chine stock, have already been beveled thirty-eight degrees, which will have to be modified slightly to fit this section of the sides. The ends of the seat must be beveled to match.

No nails nor glue is used for fastening the seats, only screws (this allows easy removal of the seat for repainting). Screw them down to the top of the seat frame and to the risers, using one-and-a-quarter-inch number 10 bronze screws.

The procedure is the same for the bow and stern seat installations, with two exceptions: more beveling is required, and there are no cant frames.

The stern seat frame end cut is beveled twelve degrees, the top bevel is five degrees, and the bottom is four degrees. The chine pieces used as risers already have the required bevel here. For the bow seat frame, the end cut takes fifteen degrees, with five degrees for the top and four degrees for the bottom; use thirty degrees for the seat riser tops.

Install the foot stretchers, against which the rower braces his feet, in the positions and with the dimensions indicated on the plan. These are oak strips, glued and nailed from the outside with one-inch bronze ringed nails, as are the risers, and like them must have their fastenings pre-bored. (If you are six feet tall or over, you will have to locate the foot stretchers a little farther aft than the plan indicates.)

The breasthook in the bow, as shown on the plans, leaves a slight open gap just aft of the stem. This is structurally sound, but I prefer to make it slightly ornamental, and to my mind more shipshape, by curving its after surface with a concave cutout and fitting it right against the stem. The side cut requires a twenty-five degree bevel, and the stem fit requires forty-three degrees. Make the breasthook of three-quarter-inch oak, and fasten it with two one-inch bronze nails on each side—marking their locations so your gunwale fastenings won't run into them.

Now you can remove your temporary spreader, and go on to the gunwales.

Cut the gunwales from oak to measure one and one-half inches by three-quarters of an inch by sixteen feet. You can put these on as the plan shows, square-edged on the bottom and rounded on the outside of the upper

With the cant frames glued and fastened to the sides, the midframe can be tied together with wood screws from forward.

Because of the way the angles converge, the stern seat-frame and risers require care in their layout and bevel.

As with the risers, the foot stretchers can be made out of leftover chine stock.

The slightly modified breasthook is cut to shape on the band-saw . . .

. . . then fitted tightly against the stem. Mark where the fastenings are so as to avoid them when fastening the gunwales. (Photo by Bill Robelen 4th.)

Glue and clamp the gunwales in place, and fasten them from inside.

edge, but I prefer to cut a thirty-degree bevel on the bottom. It looks good and it also allows the gunwales to spring on much more easily. Fasten the gunwales to the sides from the inside out with one-inch bronze ringed nails spaced five or six inches apart. You pre-bore for these, naturally.

Installing the gunwales calls for quite a few clamps—sixteen is none too many, for just one side. Glue the gunwales lavishly, and starting at the bow clamp them about every foot or so. Here's another place where a helper comes in handy, but if you don't have one, prop up the after end of the gunwale on a sawhorse or something high enough so that you can start clamping at the bow and work aft, keeping the gunwale parallel with the sheer. Round off the transom top, and cut out the sculling notch; the interior of your dory is finished.

My time for reaching this stage is forty working hours, but that is with all my patterns already made and a good many of my parts prefabricated. But even starting cold, building the Gloucester light dory is not a man-killing job.

After drawing out the shape of the top of the transom, bore a two-and-a-quarter-inch hole for the sculling notch.

A quick way to rough out the shape of the transom top is with a skil saw—but only if you are careful.

FIBERGLASSING THE BOTTOM

I strongly recommend that you fiberglass the entire bottom of the boat. You can, if you wish, use fiberglass tape to cover only the edges around the chine area where the sides meet the bottom, but careful fairing along the edge to make a really good fiberglass taping job is painstaking work and so time-consuming you might as well go whole hog. And if you've used quarter-inch plywood for the bottom, you should definitely strengthen and protect the entire bottom with fiberglass.

Twelve feet of thirty-eight-inch-wide fiberglass cloth—weight is not important, but I use 10-ounce—will do the whole job, including the stem and the transom. You have a choice of resins. You can buy a gallon of polyester resin at the local hardware store, or buy lay-up resin by the drum at a boatyard at a lower per-gallon price. The store-bought type has wax in it, which makes the resin harden better because of the air-inhibiting property of the wax. I always used this, until the price went out of sight. However, besides its high price, resin with wax has another disadvantage: the wax that makes it harden so well can become a major source of frustration if you have to leave a job partly done. The resin becomes completely cured and the wax rises to the surface and must be sanded off before additional coats of resin can be applied. Use resin that has wax in it for the last coat.

The first step before covering the bottom with fiberglass is to flip the boat again, bottom up on sawhorses. Fill all the nail-set dimples with auto-body putty, round off all outside corners of the plywood, then drop the thirty-eight-inch fiberglass cloth over the hull, with one edge hanging over the side by about three inches. Brush all the wrinkles out of the cloth with your bench brush, and trim all around with scissors. Cut pieces of a size to cover the stem and the transom and put them aside for now.

Using nonoil based putty, fill all irregularities in the surface, going over it more than once if necessary, and sand the surfaces smooth.

The interior woodwork is complete, so the dory is turned upside down so that the corners and edges can be smoothed and rounded.

When temperature and humidity are right, begin the sheathing with the bottom. Smooth out all wrinkles with a brush.

After roughing it out, the shape can be worked with a chisel, a plane, a spokeshave, and wood rasps.

Three coats of resin will do the job. How you go about it will vary with the prevailing temperature and personal preference. Some of the resin manufacturers' old manuals insist that you lay a coat on the bare wood before you lay down any cloth. I think that's risky, for if you're not quick and the ambient temperature is fairly high, you can end up with a hardened, half stuck wrinkled mess that must be sanded off. The only place where I put one resin first is a vertical surface, so it will hold the cloth in place while I'm adding more resin. Otherwise, I put the cloth on dry. I use a pint of resin at a time, adding a teaspoon of hardener. I also keep about a half-pint of acetone standing by in a pint milk container with the top cut off, to plump the three-inch roller I use for an applicator in, in case I have to leave the job for any reason. For just one job it's not worth buying the acetone, but if you're going to be using resin frequently, it's cheaper to clean your rollers and brushes with it than it is to replace them. Acetone can be used over and over; use fresh acetone only for the last rinse before you put away your applicators.

Start right in the middle of the boat, pouring a good quantity of resin onto the cloth draped over the bottom and working it in fast with a three-inch roller. When the bottom is well saturated, apply pieces you cut out for the stem and the transom, letting them both overlap the bottom, and roll the resin onto them.

When that's done it's time to mix up another batch of resin and go over the whole bottom again, including the stem and transom. Pay special attention to the edge of the bottom—it sucks up more than its share of resin because of the end grain of the plywood; you can tell it's resin-thirsty by the grayish color of the cloth where the weave shows through, and the pinholes that appear in the resin.

After two liberal coats, the surface should be all one shade if you have used enough resin. If all is well, wait a while to let the resin harden. Then mix up another pint and flow that on with a brush so that it obliterates the weave of the cloth. Finished, the surface should look as if it has been varnished, with a good deep gloss.

The sooner you start sanding, the easier the job will be. As the surface dries and hardens, it will go from glossy to dull. As long as you still see glossy streaks, hold off with the sanding or you will load the sandpaper with uncured resin.

Protected by a face mask, I start with 60-grit paper in a three-inch belt sander. That takes the excess resin off fast, *but do wear the mask.* I finish the job, still using 60-grit, with a heavy-duty vibrator that takes a half sheet of sandpaper. Fair in the edge of the cloth with autobody putty or resin mixed with Cabosil to thicken it.

When all's done, mark the location of the oak skeg on the bottom. Bore through the bottom from outside with a small drill to locate the two-inch number 14 bronze screws. Butter up the skeg with bedding compound and get someone to hold it in place while you bring it up tight with the screws from the inside. Paint the boat before you fasten the seats in.

You can figure about two weeks for building the Gloucester light dory, including time for the paint to dry. I think this building time is reasonably generous. Of course, how much calendar time it will take you depends on how many hours you're able to give it each day. Two weeks of steady work seems to me a modest investment to produce a good, reliable boat, and the short building time is one of the advantages of working with plywood.

I've urged extreme caution about attempting to design a dory, even though in one way it's child's play to design one—in fact, a child with cardboard and scissors can turn out a fairly good-looking dory model.

If you undertake to design a dory, I recommend you do the same: make up a model from cardboard that's stiff enough so that it will bend in only one plane, like plywood. This will at least let you make sure that everything will go together. If you should use Phil Bolger's light dory as a guide, but wish to make it, say, a little larger, be particularly careful to retain the same degree of flare in the sides.

But personally, I'd stick with his unmodified design.

With the cloth smoothed out, begin to saturate it thoroughly, working out from the center in all directions.

The resin is easiest applied with a three-inch roller, except along the boat's sides, where a brush works better. It takes about a quart (mixed in two one-pint batches) to do the bottom and the stem and transom pieces.

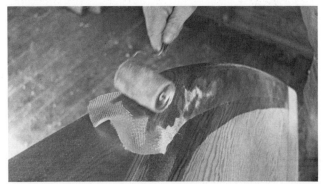
The stem and transom require an undercoat of resin on the wood so that the cloth will adhere somewhat until it is saturated in place.

When the sheathing has been sanded, the skeg is fitted to the bottom directly on the centerline and is fastened from the inside.

The final coat fills the weave of the cloth and provides a protective finish.

A first-class building job deserves a first class finish job.

16 The Thomaston Galley: Triple Treat

To me, the Phil Bolger design called the Thomaston Galley is as fascinating a boat to build and use as I have ever had the good fortune to know.

My experience with the Thomaston Galley began with the old dream of wanting a boat that I could sail, power, and row. I knew very little about sailing, except that, judging by the traffic coming and going in Muscle Ridge Channel in July, sailing had to have something going for it. I pricked up my ears when I heard a working fisherman who was also a good mechanic and an electronic technician come to sailing's defense when he was tying up his small sloop. A bystander had remarked that sailboats were slow.

The sailor turned a polite smile on the critic and said, almost in a whisper, "Yes. But what an elegant way to go."

I knew I couldn't design the paragon I had in mind, so I turned to Phil Bolger. You won't learn much about designing your own boat in this section, but you will learn just how far beyond accepted practice a drawing board wizard like Phil can go. Yet I don't recommend that you try to emulate him.

The Thomaston Galley story can teach you other valuable lessons. She was tricky to design and she is tricky to build—just about the limit in the use of plywood. Therefore, if you understand the problems she presents and how to go about meeting them, there is very little in boat-building in plywood that will baffle you. The Galley is also a good example of how to mix grained wood with the laminated variety. And as you follow me through, you will learn something about molding a fiberglass boat from an existing hull.

One reason I chose Phil Bolger to design my "triple treat" boat was the fact that he takes a very active interest in small boats and gives them as much respectful attention as he does to much larger (and more profitable) commissions. Bolger had redesigned the British frigate HMS *Rose*—a three-masted square-rigger—and had turned out dozens of trail-breaking models in the major yacht classes, yet he has also drawn an eight-foot punt for me to build.

One day when Bolger came to my shop to pick up *Kotick*, a strip-planked kayak I had built for him, I asked him why he bothered with such tiny craft when there could hardly be a nickel in it for him.

He looked at me over his pipe. "When I get to the Pearly Gates and Saint Peter asks me 'What's your ex-cuse?', I'll just say 'I was a designer of small boats.' And he'll *have* to let me in."

I asked for a fifteen- to sixteen-foot daysailer that could take whatever the weather might bring, that would row as well as his light dory design so that a dead calm wouldn't stymie me, and that would power nicely with a small outboard if I didn't have time to row. I stipulated a spritsail rig, because I was familiar with it and it is a very forgiving rig (it has several times forgiven me).

As I waited for Bolger to design the boat, my mind drew pictures of a nicely proportioned round-bottom boat with a centerboard, looking very much like the conventionally attractive daysailers that the average professional designer draws.

The waiting period wasn't long. Only a couple of

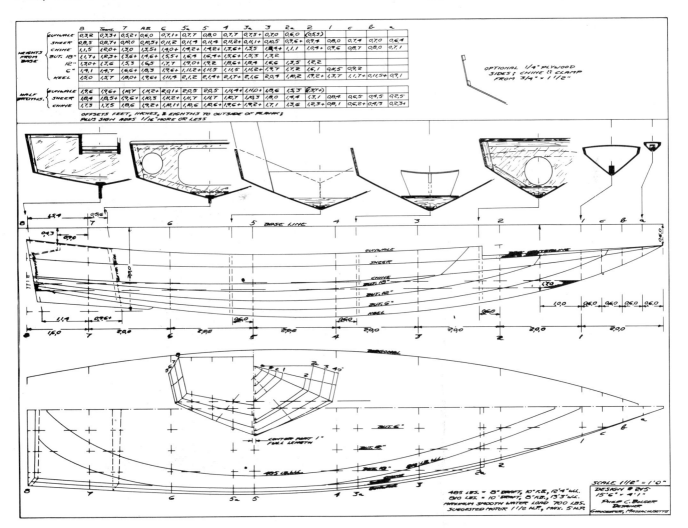

Builder's table of offsets for the Thomaston Galley.

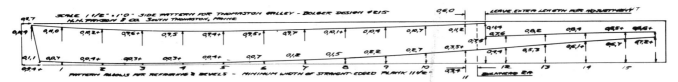

Expanded side pattern for the Thomaston Galley.

weeks after I talked to Phil, my wife, Amy, raised me on the CB in my lobster boat with: "Your plans are here—and wait till you see them!"

At the first sight of the drawings for this V-bottomed, needle-nosed craft with a foredeck that reminded me of my shop anvil, my immediate reaction was that it was the strangest looking boat I had ever seen. My second reaction was: "I'll bet he has a reason for all of it."

Considering the curves Phil Bolger had managed to wangle out of plywood, the lengthy table of offsets, and the building-jig drawings, the boat clearly wasn't going to be an easy job to build. As for appearance, I closed my eyes to that and concentrated on her functional qualities:

Roominess: eight feet of unencumbered cockpit through her full width; plenty of room for a couple to sprawl in, or even sleep in overnight with a shelter; and no problem for the solo sailor who must move his weight around quickly to balance her.

Light weight: with her quarter-inch plywood deadrise and cedar sides, she would add up to a little over a hundred pounds, and would be easily car-toppable.

Rowing ease: Bolger had noted that "the way she is balanced for windage will save a tremendous amount of energy in strong breezes—you won't have to put all your strength into keeping her straight." Which proved true.

Power: "Three horsepower will drive her easily," Bolger had written. "Note that the motor will be mounted

Thomaston Galley sailing off Spruce Head, Maine. Note that the mitre cut in sail is exactly opposite from the designer's. My mistake was picking a sailmaker who's shop was too close to the local bar. (Photo by Wilma Huntley.)

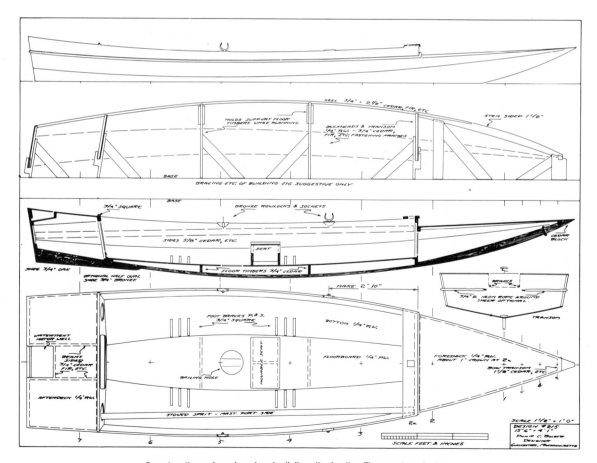

Construction plan showing building jig for the Thomaston Galley.

70

over a self-draining well so no oil will seep into the boat." Which also proved true.

Handy rig: the spritsail I'd asked for was a large quadrilateral, but both the mast and the sprit which held up the peak of the sail were the lightest of spars and both short enough to stow aboard handily.

In short, the longer I looked the better I liked her. I could see that the high, wide transom would give her powerful quarters when she was heeled, and that the flare at the bow would do the same forward. Yet her wetted surface was low and drag would be minimal.

And while the leeboard at first turned me off a little aesthetically, its benefits have far outweighed any deficiency in the beauty department. In the first place, it eliminates the nuisance of a centerboard trunk, which is always in the way in terms of both the crew's comfort and the need for quick action. The leeboard also lets you see any accumulation of rockwood or eelgrass that might foul it, and you can clear the board easily by picking the stuff off. And if the leeboard is really jammed full, all you need do is ease the sheet to relieve the strain on the board so that you can pick it up or shake it and float the junk away. Try that with a centerboard.

The more closely I studied the details of the Galley the more I wanted to build it. Anyway, it would have been a cop-out for me to walk away from the boat after Phil had gone to the trouble of designing it.

A soft ride in a hard breeze. (Photo by the author.)

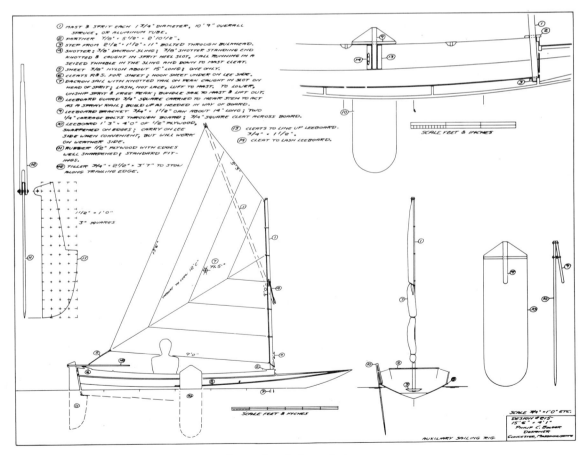

Thomaston Galley sail plan.

Not until years later did I discover that Phil had pretty well foreseen my first reaction. When his book *Small Boats* (Camden, Me.: International Marine Publishing Co., 1973) came out, I found that one chapter had been devoted to the Galley design, and that in it he had written: "Harold took his courage in both hands and built one."

Actually, what I took in both hands was Bolger's set of plans, and I studied them for days before I touched pencil, wood, or tool. And because it's all-important, I'll say it again: Even if you have drawn the plans yourself, sit down and brood over them, building the boat in your head. Don't dash out panting to your shop and plunge in blind, hoping that luck will see you through.

My procedure consists of studying what I think of as one clump of data at a time, concentrating on a single area, feature, or problem. When I have mastered such a clump, as I call it, I put it out of my head and focus my concentration on the next concern. I think the study of plans is best done in a succession of focuses like that, rather than attempting to absorb everything all at once. There is less chance of overlooking something that could mean big trouble later on.

For now, let's concentrate on the two sheets of drawings that present the jig set-up and the construction plan, and the lines and the table of offsets. All the information you need—and you need it all in order to en-sure an accurate, cleanly faired hull—is right on those two sheets.

A word of caution about accuracy—don't overdo it. Phil Bolger disposes of the common misconception that boat-building requires absolute accuracy very succinctly: "Airplanes have to be built accurate, boats don't. I ask only that the lines be fair."

This doesn't mean that you can dismiss errors with careless laughter. Phil was talking about the kind of obsession with hairline accuracy that could drive the boatbuilder to the verge of a nervous breakdown when he finds that some line he's been working with is off an eighth of an inch. The designer does his level best to see that the lines are accurate as drawn. But even with the one-and-one-half-inch-equals-one-foot scale used on the Galley plans, the designer can be off a small fraction here and there.

It is up to the builder—and it always has been—to catch such minor inaccuracies, deal with them, and keep his cool in the process. One of the ways by which the practical builder irons out small deviations in design is by the use of a batten in the lofting process. Instead of showing up as quick places or a flat effect in an otherwise fair curve, these little inaccuracies are absorbed by keeping the designed line as close as possible to the tabulated off-set figures. Let your eye be the final judge.

17 Lofting the Thomaston Galley

Boats are individuals, just as designers and builders are. Some require a lot of lofting, others none at all. Given a set of plans, it is up to the builder to decide which lines are which, and just how much lofting is called for, between the extremes of too much and too little, in order to turn a set of drawings and figures into an actual boat.

A number of books treat the subject of lofting. Howard A. Chapelle's *Boatbuilding* (New York: Norton, 1941) covers it very well. Just from reading the first few pages of the section devoted to the subject, the beginner can get the essentials for lofting some of the simpler hull forms. Chapelle then proceeds to much more complex applications, such as lofting the raked and curved transom, and on to procedures that are just about as intricate and recondite as one can imagine. Glenn L. Witt's *Boatbuilding with Plywood* (Bellflower, Calif.: Glen L., 1967) also provides clear instructions on lofting procedure, and successfully translates naval architect's lingo into layman's language to make lofting understandable to the novice.

What you'll get from me are the basics you need in order to know what to look for and where to look for it when lofting a boat like the Galley.

Three views are presented on the lines plan of the Thomaston Galley; they are called the Profile, the Plan, and the Body views, and are so designated on all sets of plans for all types of vessels:

The profile, or broad-on view from the side, lets you take any true measurement of heights above the baseline.
The plan, or bird's- or fish-eye view looking straight through one half of the hull from above or below, which lets you extract half-breadth horizontal measurements out from the centerline.
The body, or sectional view, looking through the hull from the bow aft and from the transom forward to the widest station, again in terms of half the boat. This view gives you measurements both vertically from the baseline and transversely from the centerline.

If the designer has been accurate, all three views are

in agreement wherever they have measurements in common. The builder proves or disproves the designer's accuracy (or his own) in the small details when he lays down the lines full-size for building.

Lofting is a straightforward matter of consulting the table of offsets to establish the location of significant points. Note that each column of figures in the tabulation represents a specific section of the hull, in this case starting with *a*, *b*, and *c* at the bow and proceeding from station 1 through station 8. The same numbers are indicated on the pro, plan, and body views. Remember: all heights to gunwale, sheer, chine, and other vertically measured elements are taken from the baseline; all horizontals are taken from the centerline.

Another set of lines—the buttock lines—are identified as six-inch, twelve-inch, and eighteen-inch buttocks on the profile and plan views, and also appear unlabeled in the section or body view. You will notice, if you put a straight-edge to the bottom section view, that there is a slight transverse curve from keel to chine. When you pick up the buttock measurements of the height above baseline at each station, you establish a point of this curve at that station.

Now for the practical considerations of lofting full-size: how much space will you need, and on what will you draw your full-size lines?

If you laid down your lines as the designer did on his drawings, you would need an area of at least twelve feet by sixteen feet—an awkward spread for lining up stations, squaring off buttocks, and so on. It's much better to use a space half that wide and superimpose the lines for easier reference and less crawling around. Use a pencil of one color for your profile lines and another color for your plan lines, and then—to avoid the mad jumble that superimposing more lines over both these would produce—draw the body lines separately, somewhere else.

My friend Walter Simmons does his lofting on Homesote board; other builders sweep the shop floor and lay a coat of paint over the area they use for lofting.

I loft on plywood sheets and, as with the improvised drafting tables I recommended for drawing molds for the light dory, I place the sheets on two-by-fours laid between sawhorses so the work doesn't become a hands-and-knees job. For one thing, plywood is already absolutely square to start with, which simplifies your measuring. For another, you can stand the plywood sheet up against the wall and step back to see what you've done. Walter Simmons starts that way with his sheets of Homesote, working blackboard style. As Walter points out, this keeps you from becoming a human eraser as you crawl and walk all over your loftwork when it's done flat on the floor.

Give each plywood sheet a coat of paint to draw on. I've used light gray, flat white, and semigloss white. Flat paint wears out your pencil lead very quickly; semigloss requires more pressure to put a line down. Take your pick. Or try Walter's Homesote; I think I will on my next boat. Homesote has been around a long time; it's gray and looks like pressed cardboard; it's cheaper than

plywood; and Walter says that nailholes in it seem to be self-sealing. If you want to do your lofting at floor level, Homesote will certainly be easier on your knees than plywood or the shop floor.

Let's assume you use two four-by-eight-foot sheets of plywood for your lofting. For tools you'll want a light hammer, a steel retractable tape, pencils, an awl, some wooden battens, and paint, along with one-inch number 18 or so wire brads; you may want to use a chalkline, a two-foot framing square, and dividers.

Begin by butting your sheets together. Place them end-to-end on the floor or on horses and tack them down so they can't move. When they're painted and ready to go, cut a sixteen-foot-long batten, two or three inches by a half-inch in cross-section, as straight and true as you can make it. If you have a sixteen-foot sheet of plywood, edges cut off that will be fine. Tack the batten right along and flush with the bottom edges of the two sheets of plywood and draw a line on its inboard edge. This is your baseline, where all the action starts.

Carefully draw in all the reference points and station numbers from *a* through station number 8 on your baseline, spacing them to match the distances indicated on the profile plan, and duplicate these marks on the opposite, or upper, edges of the two sheets. Then extend these marks as lines, using a straight-edge to connect the reference points. You don't have to use a square, because your plywood sheet is cut absolutely on the square. Mark each line plainly so you can easily identify the station you're working with as you proceed.

You are ready now to transfer measurements from the table of offsets. These measurements are always expressed in three figures; feet, inches, and eighths-of-an-inch, as we've discussed before. Begin with the profile, and locate the points indicated by the height-above-base-

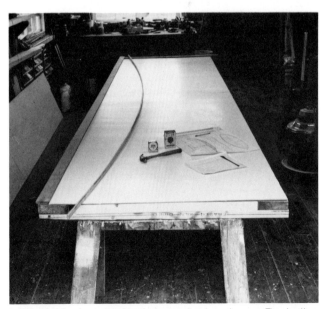

Lofting table: two sheets of plywood set on horses. The batten on the left tacked to the plywood represents the baseline. Curved batten is for drawing in the sheer and other curves. (Photo by the author.)

line figures as tabulated. You'll note that there is no height given for the gunwale at *a, b, c,* and station number 1, because there is no gunwale at any of those locations; however, there is a height listed for station number 2, even though the gunwale actually begins only at station number 2a, where the forward bulkhead is. The station number 2 reference point is there only to spot the location of a nail that will prevent your batten from going flat at the end when you're drawing the curve of the gunwale. As you locate each reference point, drive a brad right on the mark.

Carry out this process for the sheer, the chine, the buttocks, and the keel. This completes your work with the profile plan.

Start drawing your lines with the gunwale. Cut a batten long enough to extend beyond the edges of the lofting sheets by a foot or so—a batten that is at least eighteen feet long, for this boat, and which in cross-section should be about three-eighths inch by one inch. For the gunwale, which has a gentle curve, bend the batten on the flat; this will guarantee a fairer curve than you would get with a three-eighths-inch square batten, whose limberness might allow it to snake slightly. Battens sometimes seem to have minds of their own, and can be very reluctant to conform to the designer's measurements without some persuasion.

Always crowd the batten right against the nails, allowing its extra length to extend beyond the terminal nail at each end. Note how many nails the batten lies snugly against, and how far it is lying off the others, if at all—always keeping a sharp eye on the sweep of the curve. Push the batten in against the nails it doesn't touch, and see what effect this has on the batten's curve. If there is a quick place, pull a few nails here and there until the batten does form a fair curve, and drive them back in again alongside the batten.

To make sure you haven't flattened the curve at the ends, overspring the ends of the batten until it moves clear of the nails, then ease it back to make sure that it does rest against every one of the nails. Then drive the end nails to hold the batten in place, and give it one more eyeball check for fairness. At no time in this process do you ever drive a nail through the batten.

You're ready now to lay off the half-breadth distances for the plan view. The baseline is now the centerline, and you butt your rule against the batten fastened on the edge of your plywood just as before. Sweep in the curves of the gunwale, sheer, and chine with the batten, just as you did for the profile. Bolger has drawn in two load waterlines, one for four hundred eighty-five pounds and one for eight hundred ten pounds, but you don't need to think about these while lofting. You can, if you wish, establish the heights of these lines above the baseline, and their half-breadths from the centerline by scaling these from the plan, thus giving yourself additional reference points by which to check your accuracy.

Now draw in the body sections, which will give you the shapes of the bulkheads, the transom, and the jig molds 5a and 3a—six pieces in all. Check these cross-sections against the jig set-up indicated and note where they will fall when you make the jig.

Using your original baseline and any one of the perpendiculars that strikes your fancy as the centerline, lay out one of these sections, but don't overlook the point of intersection of the buttock line.

If at this point you wonder why you didn't skip all the preceding lofting and go straight to this stage, don't. Every step of the process is necessary to make certain that each component will go where it should, and that the sum of all of them will make up the hull the designer drew, fair and true.

As is customary, your Galley plans are drawn to the "outside of planking"; therefore you now reduce the sides and bottoms of each section to allow for the thickness of planking. This means taking a quarter-inch off the bottoms and five-eighths of an inch off the sides if you build the boat as I do, using five-eighths-inch grained wood for the sides and nailing the quarter-inch plywood bottom to them. This does away with the work of fitting in a chine, which would be required if you chose the option of using quarter-inch plywood for the sides.

To make these reductions, use your dividers, set to the thickness to be taken off, and with their point set on the lines, swing a series of arcs; drive a brad in at the highest tangent of each little arc, to make sure that you are marking the full thickness of the reduction you wish to make. Use a batten to sweep in the same degree of curve that your untrimmed bottom had between the chine and the keel. A straight-edge will do for the sides, since they have no curve.

At this point I sense a nervous twitch from purists, who are apt to point out that the only place you can determine true plank thickness by this method is right amidships, where there is no bevel in the mold station, and that as the bevel will increase at each forward and after section, so too will the amount of plank thickness to be taken off. I hope to be forgiven for calling this nitpicking. For one thing, the side plank you're going to wrap around the skeleton is probably already cupped slightly, as was discussed earlier in regard to carvel planking. For another, this is a boat you're building, not a temple to the god of split hairs. So don't worry about it.

You must also take a quarter-inch from the transom and the after bulkhead to allow for the thickness of the afterdeck, which is included as a part of the gunwale you lofted. Keep the two quarter-inch slices you have cut off here, and tack them back on when you set them up on the jig, to maintain the curve you developed in this area. Of course, you can leave the quarter-inch on until it's time to lay down the afterdeck, but it's easier to cut it away now.

Up forward, instead of butting the foredeck against the nose block as shown in the plan, I cut down the block to let the deck cover it. That nose block looked quite vulnerable to me, and remembering that Phil Bolger had said it would be my fault if it broke off, I thought it only fair, and prudent, to cut it down in advance. Now is the time to work out the bevels for the framing of the bulkheads to which you will nail the bottom and the sides. Take them right off your lofted lines and write them on your paper templates where they'll be handy when you saw out the frames. Also, mark out the keel notch for each bulkhead, and put down the bevel each notch will require.

Lay out the height of the two floor timbers to which the bottom will be nailed at the stations called 5a and 3a on the offset table, and leave slots for them in the molds at these two positions; just shove a board through the slots and mark the bottom shape from the molds around them. These floor timbers must go into the jig before the keel goes in, and they are notched to fit the keel.

Since the stem is sided one and one-half inches, both it and the bow transom can be cut from pieces of two-by-fours.

SETTING UP THE JIG

With one exception, I followed Phil Bolger's specifications for the jig as indicated on the plan. I used a piece of two-by-six set on edge and bolted to the transverse two-by-fours, which worked out to give just the proper height to permit me to rest the bow transom and stem on the jig.

Quite a lot of fine tuning is required to get the jig set up properly; it must be lined up in relation to the cen-

terlines, as you'll recall from the earlier chapter on building the Gloucester light dory, and once it is exactly in place the jig must be solidly fastened down. If it isn't, you'll know it when you try to bend a cedar side plank around it and find the whole rig is waltzing across the floor.

If you go overboard in building up the bracing, you may have trouble snapping a chalk line to check alignment with your centerlines. However, there is a solution to this problem, provided you have picked only the straightest of two-by-fours and have been careful to space them equally, as the plan requires, from the bulkhead centerlines—the long side pieces or runners on which the rest of the jig sits. Take a short piece of board that is about three inches wide, and split it into three pieces. Nail one of these pieces at each end of the two-by-four whose ends have already been fastened to the floor. Then drive a nail part way into each piece and stretch a chalk line between them. Now, using the third piece of board as a feeler gauge held between the string and the runner, move the center of the jig in and out sideways until the gap is the same in the middle as it is at the ends.

All set? Nail her down, and let's go on to getting out the cedar side pieces and covering her in.

From top to bottom: Stem, transom, after bulkhead, and forward bulkhead of the Thomaston galley framed and beveled with keel notches cut, ready to accept keel. (Photo by the author.)

Jig set-up, with keel and stem in place. Battens are tacked along the chine and sheer, ready for taking off shape of side. (Photo by the author.)

18 The Thomaston Galley: Planking Up

You are about to find out just how accurately you have been working. With your bulkheads, transom, stem, and bow transom all in place, you can take off a pattern for the two side pieces.

Just as with the Gloucester light dory, spring battens along the chine and the sheer of the Thomaston Galley. Let me interject here a wrinkle I use when springing a batten to take off a side pattern on an upside-down hull like this, if the hull has a sharp hook to the sheer in the after area: to make sure the batten curve maintains a nice, fair sweep, I hang a weight on the end of the batten that protrudes beyond the transom, to keep it pulled down edgewise. This procedure is not necessary on the Galley hull, but you can try it to see how it works, and file it away for future reference.

Do both battens hit all the marks they're supposed to? When you step back, do they reproduce the nice, fair curves in the designer's drawing?

If the answer is "yes," congratulate yourself, and drink from the Cup of Victory.

If you are going to get the sides out of straight boards, you will first want to know how wide they must be. Therefore, lay your paper side pattern up against a straight seam on your shop floor, with both ends of the gunwale touching the seam; then measure from the middle of the seam to the belly of the side pattern.

In this case you'll find that the minimum width of the side is eleven and a quarter inches. You will also find, if you don't already know it, that eleven or twelve-inch planks sixteen feet long aren't easy to come by in the average lumberyard. I happen to be blessed by the presence of the Rockland Boat Shop only a dozen miles away, and Morse's Boat Shop in Thomaston practically in my backyard. I had my first Thomaston Galley sides sawed from Philippine mahogany by Roger Morse, who knocked off working on one of those millionaire's yachts he turns out to get right on the end of that plank and ride it right through the planer, where he and I both got buried in the shavings in the discharge end. And one time when I was standing first in line at the Newbert and Wallace yard in Thomaston, waiting to have some oak planed down—only to find that the boys dropped everything to come to the assistance of a nice-looking woman who needed a special piece of wood for a sculpture—Herbert Newbert came down from the loft and said: "Has that fellow been taken care of?" Getting a shaky "No," he snapped out: "Around here, boatbuilders come first," and stomped back up to the loft.

That mahogany cost me seventy cents a foot. A year later it was over a dollar, and the last time I checked it was two and a half dollars a foot and climbing. I now use cedar.

You may lose money in terms of the value of your time, but with cedar you achieve lighter weight in your topsides. Also, for the Thomaston Galley, the natural shape of the plank will match the curve of the sides. And personally I prefer working cedar to working mahogany.

Granted, with mahogany you don't have to contend with the knots and gray rot of cedar, but you still have to keep a sharp eye out for swirly grain, and sometimes even cross grain that loves to snap in two when you have the plank just about fastened in place. So I'll stick with cedar as long as I can get it, and use mahogany only if I must.

While it is no problem finding enough live-edged cedar boards with the right sweep to match the side panels for the Thomaston Galley, width is another matter. I pick up a couple of planks and add strips to one edge to widen them out. To do this, I place the side pattern on the plank and mark off the bottom or chine curve along its full length, and then mark off the top of the sheer forward from section 2a, since the Galley is quite skinny there. Next, I pull the pattern down far enough to mark the top of the gunwale on the wood that is left on the plank. Following this, I place the pattern down on the mark drawn around it for the chine, and measure from the gunwale I have just drawn to the top of the gunwale on the pattern. That's the width I need to fill the space on my side planks. I then cut a couple of parallel strips of cedar, glue and edge-nail them to the gunwale, and I have my side plank.

The two-and-a-half-by-three-quarter-inch keel should go on first, before the sides are fastened in place, because it is easier to work on the keel without having the sides in the way. Cut the keel from spruce, pine, or whatever, to a length of twelve feet six inches, and slip it into the notches pre-cut in the molds from the transom on forward to where it ends in the scarph joint of the stem. To establish the bevel for the keel, there must be a centerline on both the keel and stem. First, put the keel in square-edged; then since the bevel changes from very little at the transom to a lot at the stem, fair in the bevel from the keel's centerline to fit each mold station, and then in between the stations.

In general, it is a good idea to bevel boat components before putting them into a hull. For example, the angle between the sides and the bottom at the transom of the Thomaston Galley is twenty-three degrees, and I cut that bevel the entire length of the edge of the plank without any hesitation to start with, because its angle gets progressively sharper. This saves a lot of unnecessary work later; it assures me that the bottom plywood will land on the transom at just the right angle, and as I work forward I can establish the changing bevel between the sides and the bottom very much in the way I establish the bevels of the planking on a round-bottom boat. Here, however, instead of using a small bevel square, I spring a thin batten from the keel—which at this stage has already been at least roughly beveled—and across the edge of the side plank, cutting a notch in the latter to the depth indicated by the batten. I then run all these notches together in a fair curve with a hand plane. If you don't trust your eye to this extent, spring a batten along the notches and draw a line, down to which you will plane. Make sure you don't take even a whisker off the inside edge of the plank, for the curve of the inside edge is what the bottom will follow, and to cut into it would produce a snake-like juncture where the bottom meets the sides.

Now back to the keel. I've tried the short-cut method of pre-beveling it, which showed me how easy it is to make a mistake. I put the same twenty-three degree bevel on the keel as I had on the sides, and although it looked right, I had forgotten that the keel is on the flat and the sides are on edge.

That's right—I had over-beveled the keel by easily twice as much as required, and it showed up right away when I plopped it in place. I hung that nice, clear piece of keel in plain sight on the shop wall as a monument to stupidity and waste.

So, with your correctly beveled keel in place, bend the sides around very carefully, making sure they hit all the chine marks. If there is any unevenness, make·sure it turns up on what will be the top edge of the plank. Because these wide side planks cannot be edge-set, as a narrow plank in a carvel-planked hull could be edge-set simply by pounding it down to make wood-to-wood contact with the plank below, the chine marks on the jig molds bulkheads must coincide with those on the sides. If you were careful in making your side pattern, they will coincide.

Wrap one side around, and when you're satisfied that it's ready to be nailed, slip a stick across the jig at the midpoint of the boat, right under the sheer, and clamp it there. Now clamp the side in place at the stern, the bow, and at bulkhead 2a. With that much clamping, you can remove the transom clamp in preparation for gluing and fastening, without any fear that the side might slip a little at the forward end. When the plank springs free from the transom, the stick you clamped under the sheer will help support the weight.

Now apply glue to the framing of the transom and the after bulkhead, and reclamp the side to the transom. Before you do any nailing, take a stroll along the entire length of the boat and inspect it to make sure the side plank hasn't slipped anywhere, in any direction.

Nail the side to the transom and the after bulkhead with inch-and-a-quarter anchorfast nails and wipe off any excess glue; then fasten the forward part of the plank. Don't worry about the after end you just nailed; it isn't going anywhere. Repeat this process on the other side, and your side planking is finished.

Now fair the keel down to match the chine bevels, and you're ready to put on the bottom sheet of quarter-inch plywood. Begin by dividing the sixteen-foot-long sheet lengthwise, right down the middle.

Working alone, you'll find these two bottom pieces difficult to handle. You can, if you wish, make a rough bottom pattern out of lengths of light plywood scrap; but if this seems too time-consuming, just rough-shape your

Live-edged planks were picked to match the curve of the side pattern. Strips have been glued and nailed to edges at the sheer to gain width. (Photo by the author.)

Sides are notched and the cuts faired with a batten to accept the ever changing twist of the bottom. Skills learned in carvel planking are used again here. (Photo by the author.)

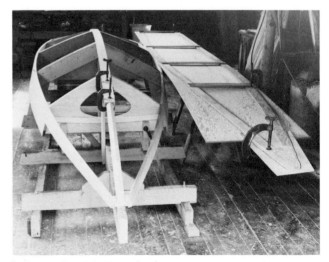

Bottom pattern is laid out on sheet and marked around for cutting. (Photo by the author.)

77

bottom pieces, cut and hack style.

You'll find that the half-sheet allotted to each bottom piece isn't quite wide enough to go all the way from the outer edge of the side plank to the centerline of the keel amidships; there will be a very slight gap along a length of about three feet. However, there is plenty of wood left forward and aft of the gap which you can add on to the bottom piece. Simply fill the gap with a sliver of this extra plywood covered with glue; this will be required on both the two bottom pieces. In order to shorten this gap at the keel, keep the plywood edge that is nailed to the cedar side eased as far inboard as possible, without introducing a gap there.

Once a bottom piece is in place, it will cover the framing into which you will have to drive nails; therefore, first mark your bottom so that you can locate the nails properly. At each bulkhead, floor timber, and other locations that must accept nails, put a center mark on both the keel and the side plank; then use a batten to make sure that the nails will hit paydirt if they're driven in on a line between the marks. Because the bottom has some transverse curve, a straight batten will curve a little, too. With the bottom in place, draw a line across it along the batten, connecting the keel and side-plank marks; this will be your nailing guideline.

Place the bottom sheet on, allowing a slight overhang at both ends; adjust it for the best fit all around; and tack it down here and there so that it won't move when you drive in the permanent nails. Do your final fitting with as little overhang as you dare, because the fastenings up forward—where the angle between bottom and sides is most severe—are tricky and can easily throw your eye off. Even though I have built more than a dozen Galleys, and know what to expect, I still sometimes manage to miss the frame underneath and put a nail through the plank instead, up forward. I would say that Phil Bolger approached the limit of the angle at which you can nail such a joint together; any more, and he would have had to design a different joint system.

You've probably noticed that the plywood bottom piece doesn't want to conform to the rocker between the chine and the keel, slight as it is, but instead develops a cup in the wrong direction, just enough to make nailing it even more difficult. Give that spot a sponge bath with warm water. (If you have a stove in your shop, keep a bucket of water on it all the time for just such occasions.) On plywood as thin as this, it doesn't take long to swell the outside this way, and it will soon lie just as desired, without further protest. Or, if you live in a warm climate, throw the plywood out on the ground in the sun, with the side you want to have swell facing down. Damp ground speeds the swelling, and a hot sun will shrink the upper side at the same time. You can admire this silent and efficient process while you sit in the shade with a cool beer. Fifteen or twenty minutes will do it. Now take the bottom sheets into the shop, slather glue on everything to which they will be fastened, and nail them on.

After this is completed, and the glue is dry, remove her from the jig (she's a boat now, and entitled to be called "her") and set her, still upside down, on a couple of sawhorses. Fill the nailheads and any other imperfections with auto-body filler or any other compound that is compatible with polyester resin, then round off the corners at the chine and transom, and reduce the keel to a width of one inch along its entire length.

Form the nose block from a piece of spruce, mahogany, cedar, or whatever. If you don't have stock that is thick enough, use a couple of pieces glued together, roughed to the approximate shape of the nose block. Glue and nail it to the bow transom and let the glue harden overnight. Next day, work it down fair with the sides and the bottom.

Glass the boat's seams with three-inch fiberglass tape, following the procedure described for the light dory. The nose, however, needs special attention. Glass it right down to the tip end of the nose block, letting each course of tape along the chines and the bottom overlap at the nose. With three layers of tape on the bottom and the overlap of the deck on the top, you won't have to worry about the nose breaking free where it is butted against the bow transom.

With the glassing completed, fasten the skeg just as described for the dory. Because the skeg tapers down to nothing, add a brass or bronze half-oval strip for protection. Offset the forward end of the strip a little so that it buries in the wood and won't catch on obstructions. I didn't do that with my first Galley, and I got quite a jolt when I hauled her up on a float and the bronze strip came up against the edge.

When you turn your Galley right side up, you'll find that one of her peculiarities is a disinclination to be handled, with no gunwale guard or any other feature you can get a grip on, she'll slip right away from you every time. Then, too, with that rockered V-bottom, she doesn't like to lie where you put her, either, so I suggest you build a small cradle to hold her while you're finishing the top. She will be quite docile in that.

Unless you're blessed with four-foot arms, install the bow eye *before* you put on the deck. Since the spray guards are nailed from the inside, the deck will have to wait until you've installed them, too.

Where the guards start—aft, by the leeboard, right in the middle of the bend of the sides—they are difficult to hold. So I use a screw at this point and, working along forward toward the bow, I fasten the guards on with anchor nails for the rest of their length, using pre-bored holes.

Now for the foredeck. The crowned deck support is fastened to the bulkhead. Although the plans don't call for it, I have added a one-and-one-quarter-inch-by-three-quarter-inch strongback, which is fastened to the deck support and is carried on through to the bow transom. It isn't needed to supply additional support for the deck—the crown curve of the deck itself provides plenty of strength. But for some reason, in the very first Galley I built, the deck crown viewed in profile took on a very unlovely reverse curve, and in every Galley I have built since, I have installed the strongback to eliminate this.

The motor well is next, braced as shown, after which you can lay the afterdeck, letting it into the sides by its own thickness, following the line of the gunwale. To do this, set your combination square for a quarter-inch depth and scribe the deck thickness along the gunwale. Next, make a series of cuts about two inches apart, down to this line, with a handsaw. Use a drawknife to remove the excess wood between the cuts, being mindful of the pattern of the grain. Finish the cut with a block plane and rasp, or use a chisel if you like.

If you took a quarter-inch off the tops of the transom and the after bulkheads during the lofting process, you're all set. If you didn't (and I confess that I have forgotten to do this on occasion), then you must take these tops down now, just as you did the sides. When you've done this by hand, the hard way, a few times (assuming you're going in for Galley-building in a big way), you'll soon remember to do it the easy way.

Flatten the cuts in the sides and the motor-well bracing straight across, and fit the forward edge of the deck up to the face of the after bulkhead; also, bevel the deck edge to match the angle of the bulkhead in the hull. This fit is important; you don't want to find, after cutting the hole in the deck to match your motor well, that the deck must then be moved slightly forward in order for it to come up to the after bulkhead face.

When you're certain of its fit, remove the deck and, using a straight-edge, mark the motor-well location on the sides, and fore and aft on the transom and after bulkhead. Replace the deck and put a pencil dot on the edge of the sheet and another directly on the hull. (Establish as many of these reference points as you want; it's the same idea as taking cross-bearings to establish a fix.) Again using a straight-edge, repeat the marking process for making the well cut, marking right on the plywood this time.

Cut out the well with a sabre saw or a hand power saw with a planer blade, leaving a sixteenth-inch margin inside the line. When you put the deck back on and match up the dots, it should fit perfectly.

I don't recommend chalking the edges of the well and slamming the deck down to make your cut lines on it where it picked up the chalk. Nor do I advise establishing the hole in the deck by relying on a combination square or on measurement; you may find that you have been less accurate than you thought. If you do it my way, relying on your dots—your "cross-bearings"—everything will match up. No one will even notice if the hole is out of square a sixteenth of an inch or so. I don't mean to justify sloppy work on the basis that it can be disguised by clever procedure; what I'm saying is that there is no need to waste time being super-accurate when super-accuracy isn't needed. The paying customers for whom I build boats probably appreciate the time I save this way, which otherwise might be reflected in their bills.

Your after deck is on now, and its coaming is finished; the floor board comes next. The quarter-inch specified in the plans gave me a nervous twitch when I considered the size and weight of some people I take sailing, so I made the floor board from a ten-foot-long sheet of three-eighths-inch marine plywood. Don't waste your time trying three-eighths-inch exterior plywood—it doesn't have enough plies to be adequately strong.

You can take the shape of the floor board right off the drawing with a scale rule. Establish a centerline, draw width points from that, and sweep out the curves

Bottom half planked. Note the scarph joint on the forward end of the panel; the method is described under "Scarphing Plywood." (Photo by the author.)

The Galley right side up, all corners have been glassed, taped, and sanded. The hull waits now for decks, floorboard, and mast partner. (Photo by the author.)

How to make a clamp do the job when it won't reach. Fastening the spray rail. (Photo by the author.)

with a batten. I laid my shape out on building paper and traced around the pattern onto the plywood, leaving an ample allowance for end fit. I put the specified foot stretchers in my first Galley, but thereafter I substituted a single cleat across the floor board at a distance convenient for my feet, or for the feet of the customer; the stretchers were too much work for too little gain.

The only woodworking remaining for the rowing version of the Thomaston Galley is building the movable seat. Bolger credits L. Francis Herreshoff for its basic design, and like all the products of that master yacht designer's pencil, it is simple, neat, and effective. The construction of the seat is shown in the plan and profile views, and again in the line drawing of the body section at station number 3a.

Saw the quarter-inch plywood top of the seat so that it bends cross-grain to the curve. The top bends much more easily this way, as I can testify because I once cut it the other way through sheer inattention.

Now to give the Galley her wings.

19 The Thomaston Galley: the Sailing Rig

I mentioned earlier that one of the reasons I specified the spritsail rig for the Thomaston Galley was that it is very forgiving to the inexperienced sailor. You can get away with executing flying jibes because there is no boom to mow you down or wrench the mast out of her when the wind sneaks around the after edge of the sail and whangs the whole works right around the other way. Also because there is no boom on the foot of the sail, you can dump the wind lightning fast should you find yourself overpowered, simply by letting go the sheet. Even if you were to get panicky, you would only have to let go of everything—the tiller included, and you can shut your eyes if you like—and the Galley will take care of both herself and you.

There is only one no-no: Never tie down the sheet.

There is an implied corollary to this rule, which is: make sure the sheet is never tangled up in anything, but is always free to run out.

Here in Maine, where the waters are frigid even in midsummer, it is easy to convince people that the better part of sailboat valor is to remain upright. (However, I understand that even warm water can drown you.) One builder of the Galley confessed to me that he had flipped his boat once by ignoring the sheet rule. He must have worked quite hard to tie it down, too, for the thumb cleat for the sheet is intentionally rounded at the thumb end and short, which makes it impossible to take double hitches around it.

If worst comes to worst and you somehow do manage to capsize your Galley, at least you won't get knocked out by a flying boom.

Yet, just because the rig is safe, don't underestimate its driving power. Howard Chapelle and other noted authorities on the sailing workboats of America have proved that many of the spritsail-rigged craft are handy, weatherly, and fast (as indeed they had to be, with the life as well as the livelihood of many a user depending on them). These experts have hailed the spritsail as one of the most powerful rigs for windward use, and any sailor who has used one will vouch for its wind-hugging drive.

For starters, install the mast partner—the wooden unit through which the mast is lowered when it is stepped, and which supports the mast at about gunwale level. I make this thwartships member out of spruce, usually; pine or mahogany are also suitable. I begin with a piece three-quarters of an inch thick and six inches wide, cut long enough to extend past the boat's sides. Mark it for centering with the centerline you drew on the forward bulkhead (station number 2a). On its underside, I glue and fasten a piece of quarter-inch plywood, of the same size and shape; the purpose of this is to avoid having the grained wood of the partner split, which could happen, when you are stepping or unstepping the mast and a gust of wind or a violent sea puts a wrenching strain on it. Once the partner is correctly aligned and in place, I trim off the excess that extends past the sides.

Make the leeboard and the rudder from half-inch marine plywood, or two pieces of quarter-inch marine plywood glued together. If you choose the latter approach, make each of these units the middle of a "pressure sandwich" while the glue is setting, rather than clamping the two plywood halves together directly, which results in uneven clamp pressure. To do this, after applying your epoxy glue and mating the two halves, put both the leeboard and the rudder between two heavier pieces of plywood and put the clamps to these. You will get a nice solid bond, and a glue line to be proud of.

When the glue is dry, fair both these pieces, but take particular care with the rudder. The leading edge of the rudder can be thicker than the trailing edge, but should still be nicely rounded. The trailing edge should be quite thin. If you haven't thinned it enough, it will chatter when you're sailing; you will hear and feel a kind of shaking effect.

I made the mast and the sprit both one and three-quarters of an inch square, with no taper, on my first Galley. On the sail plan, note that a short length of line called a snotter thrusts the sprit upward to lift the peak of the sail. When I put my new boat through her paces—jibing, attempting a knockdown, the works—I found that when I let go of the sheet, the snotter bound up because the square mast couldn't turn in the step, as it should to allow the whole rig to swivel around. I therefore switched to a mast with a round cross-section, and increased the diameter to two inches to offset the loss of strength suffered by the removal of wood in the rounding process. I've since taken to rounding the sprit as well as the mast, and I taper the sprit a little, too, just because it's a nice touch.

As for spar material, I'm not inclined to be fussy. Natural-grown spruce, fir, or pine is strongest, because it hasn't had slices taken through the grain. However, you can saw your spars from a plank if you can find one that is thick enough, or from an ordinary two-by-four ripped to a thickness of one inch and laminated. This means some waste, but consider the low price of a two-by-four. You can probably find a use for the scraps anyway, if only as fuel for your shop stove.

As designed, the heel of the mast is crowded up close to the forward bulkhead, and is notched to the bottom framing of that unit. But because this prevents the mast from turning in the step, I moved the mast aft (after first checking with Phil Bolger) just enough to clear the bulkhead framing.

You can make your mast step of wood, but I decided to use brass. I bored a quarter-inch hole in a piece of one-eighth-inch-by-one-and-half-inch flat brass, and screwed the step down on the keel centerline. I then took a three- or four-inch length of quarter-inch brass rod, ground one end down to a taper, and drove it into an undersized hole in the heel of the mast. I like the no-slip feel of the mast when that quarter-inch rod plunks down into its corresponding quarter-inch hole.

A hole saw of the right size does nicely for boring the mast partner. Such saws are available for several hole sizes, and can be used interchangeably on an attachment that fits a quarter-inch drill. A bargain package of half-a-dozen sizes of saws might catch your eye, but I've tried them and found them to be too flimsy to make it worthwhile lugging them home. I say: pay up and buy the cutter size you need now, and add to your saw (and other tool) collection as your pocket allows.

Your mast-fitting requirements are minimal: two cleats to hold the sling and snotter and, if you wish, a cleat for a small-diameter line to hold down the tack of the sail. The specified three-quarter-inch nylon rope sheer guard looks nice, but the space between the leeboard and the Galley's sides doesn't really allow room for it. So instead I cut a strip of wood long enough to go the whole length of the hull, and groove it for a piece of three-eighths nylon or Dacron. There's just room for the leeboard to clear such a guard.

The Thomaston Galley has given me more pleasure-filled hours than any other boat I have ever owned. I've found, too, that a wide range of people found her very appealing. In fact, I was a little surprised when a friend of mine from Matinicus Island—a dyed-in-the-wool powerboat fisherman—suffered a case of love at first

sight over her. True, I had just towed him in his skiff, under sail, faster than he could have rowed, and dropped him smartly at his private wharf. But I didn't expect him to buy her on the spot, as he did.

Another of my Galleys passed a rugged "tugboat test" one day when I towed a twenty-six-foot lobster boat whose engine had quit a quarter of a mile from the

Leeboard is in the middle of a pressure sandwich with the clamp pressure evenly distributed. (Photo by the author.)

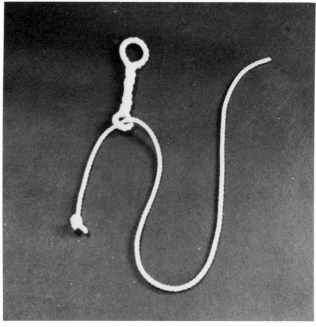

Three-eighth-inch Dacron snotter and sling. Knotted end of snotter is caught in sprit heel slot, with the fall (other end) running in a seized thimble in the sling and down to mast cleat. (Photo by the author.)

wharf. The towing produced a kind of rubber-band sensation, because I would get sailing only to have the powerboat bring me up with a jerk and start gaining on me until I got way on her again, but she and the Galley and I all made it.

The only unpleasant experience I had with a Thomaston Galley turned out to be my fault. When I put my first one out on a mooring, I found that on several occasions after a moderate amount of rain and quite a little wind, she was filled with water with her gear washed out. As I didn't live in sight of her, and so couldn't see what was happening, it was a mystery until one day I caught her turning turtle. The problem then became obvious: I always left her with the sail wrapped loosely around the mast, so when the fold of the sail filled with rain she would list over from the weight to where the wind could knock her down. Having grown tired of rowing to Norton's Island, a mile to leeward where her gear

always drifted, I thereafter made a practice of unstepping the mast every time I left her, no matter how promising the weather looked.

I was especially pleased to discover that only the slightest amount of wind was necessary to get the Galley back to the mooring, but even in a dead calm she rowed so easily that I never worried about how far I might stray from home.

I had specified a boat for sail, oars, and power, but I never got around to putting a motor on her. So when Phil Bolger asked me how she did under power, and I told him I didn't know, he tried her with an outboard. His report: "The three-horse Seagull drives her very well and she goes against a steep chop without pounding or being stopped at all."

We were both pleased as Punch.

If you've built one Galley and want another, right away, the next chapter will tell you how to clone one.

PART THREE

A MISCELLANY OF SIMPLE SOLUTIONS

There are certain problems that every boat-builder is sure to face at one time or another. Oddly, many of them are ignored in writings directed to the amateur builder. I certainly found it difficult to get really practical guidance anywhere, except in the occasional laconic mumblings of experienced old boat-builders.

I see no reason for you to clamber laboriously over the same obstacles I did. So here are some techniques I've gleaned in fragments over the years, and some I think I puzzled out for myself (although I'm sure that others have worked their way to the procedures as I have).

These are the simplest effective ways I know for accomplishing a variety of objectives. And believe me, if I ever find simple ways to do anything, I use them.

20 "Taking Her Off" In Fiberglass

At about the time I was thinking of applying for a socially acceptable job at the ill-fated fiberglass-boat plant in Rockland, it occurred to me that there would be no harm in acquiring some experience in glass layup, as the process of reproducing a shape by applying fiberglass to a mold is called. Nearby was a finished Thomaston Galley hull, without spray boards and decks—a perfect plug to play with.

Since it took me about a month to build a Galley, there was something very tempting about duplicating it in a day, which is what I figured laying up the bare hull would require.

I want to make it clear here that I'm not providing a treatise on duplicating a hull with fiberglass, nor even an example to follow. In the early 1960s, many backyard builders were inspired to experiment with the idea of producing a batch of boats by this super-easy method, and I suppose every possible variation was tried. What you *can* get from reading this is an indication of what an amateurish approach worked out by a professional wood boat-builder will accomplish; nothing more.

I don't for a minute think that you're going to take your Galley—assuming you decide to build one in the first place—and convert it to a mold for a fiberglass fleet. You may, however, at some time decide to reproduce an existing hull via the fiberglass route. If you're serious about such a project, read some of the good books devoted to the subject of building with fiberglass.

I regarded the whole venture as being possibly the supreme test of building in glass. If the product worked it would be a major victory for the material.

Speaking generally, the correct procedure calls for using a mold with a coating of mold release, a gel coat—sprayed or brushed over that—for the external skin, a couple of layers of fiberglass mat, and however many layers of woven roving, which is made up of strands of fiberglass in a kind of basket-weave form, the builder thinks necessary to achieve the strength, weight, or both that are desired.

For one thing, I detested working with mat because of its cat-hair, stick-to-everything characteristics. I began with a coating of mold release, and skipped the gel coat, used fiberglass cloth instead of mat, and depended on a very heavy thickness of woven roving to beef up the lay-up. Add to these deviations the fact that my shop provides less than laboratory conditions—with one side near the iron stove and the other next to a weather wall—and you can see that the cards were pretty well stacked against proper fiberglass construction that particular winter.

The one thing going for my experiment was the shape of the hull, which has only convex angles and curves. That made breaking the hull shell out of the mold pretty easy, with a few healthy whacks with a rubber hammer and a little water eased in between the shell and the mold.

The result was notably limber in the flat areas between the chine and the keel, and my short cuts had been duly paid for with an occasional air bubble here and there in the fiberglass. I left the hull outdoors all summer while occasionally taking time out to balance figures in my head—such as how much time I had already expended, how much I had paid for resin or spent for cloth, the amount of work required to stiffen her,

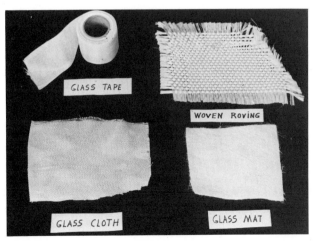

Four types of fiberglass commonly used. (Photo by the author.)

and the additional investment in materials that the stiffening would call for.

I finally decided to make a boat of it, so back into the shop it went. I applied more cloth in the cockpit area, put in wooden bulkheads and plywood strengthening pieces to bolster the sides, put in decks and spray guards, and added more weight—with the result that the hull climbed from the standard Galley's one hundred thirty pounds to the neighborhood of two hundred.

I had no intention of trying to sell the glass Galley, for the whole job was less than first class, and the basket weave of the woven roving showed right through the paint. However, I did want to give the boat the use test to see if I could have enough confidence in fiberglass to add it to my repertory if I ever wanted to build in glass professionally. If my boat didn't fall apart, there was hope.

In the end I sailed that concoction for years, with no problems. True, when she was new she would emit a few creaking protests if some heavy-footed passenger stepped on a thin spot, generating a spiderweb of hairline cracks radiating from the point of impact. But there was no real damage.

Still, there were several things about the feel of her that I didn't like. It was necessary to sit on cushions right on the bottom, and when there was a cushion shortage, sitting on the bare hull was like leaning against the damp side of my picture window. It also took me a while to get used to seeing sunlight through the hull when she was heeled, and watching water rushing by only a thin skin away. (These disquieting features can of course be avoided by using a color-impregnated gel coat.) Eventually I did sell her, but only to a friend who understood the boat's idiosyncrasies.

So much for the fiberglass boat-building career of H. H. Payson—to date, at least.

21 Tools and Their Maintenance

You don't need an impressive battery of tools to build small boats, either planked-up or of plywood. What is important is the condition you keep them in.

My shop is completely lacking in such heavy tools as a thickness planer, an oversize bandsaw, a joiner, or anything else that can't be moved around to make room for my projects. I still get all my thickness planing done at a boatyard. My own tool collection consists of a small bandsaw, a table saw, a hand power saw, a belt sander, a grinding wheel, electric hand drills, and a bit more, which takes care of all my power tool needs. The rest is easy—that is, if you know how to sharpen your own tools and understand what's going wrong when they refuse to cut just how and where you want them to.

Some builders are lucky in that they can afford to throw away most of their dull saw blades, and therefore don't have to understand what makes them work. The blades of their hacksaw, coping saw, sabre saw, tempered band saw, and table saw are all as disposable as Kleenex. However, chisels, plane knives or blades, good hand saws, and other quality-edged hand tools can't be thrown away so casually, and the builder should at least learn to sharpen those he uses—and therefore dulls—every day. I have a small, low-angle block plane that I have been using, dulling, and sharpening for twenty years.

My bench whetstone, coarse on one side and fine on the other, is what I mostly use to care for my edges. Every sharpening begins with an an application of kerosene, for if the stone isn't loaded with this, it will glaze over. Instead of taking an edge, the blade or knife will then just slide over the stone, and nothing will be accomplished other than a little healthy exercise for the wrist and fingers. The function of the kerosene is not to lubricate; it is there to float off the particles of metal ground away by the stone, which would otherwise clog the stone's pores and destroy its abrasive surface. You can buy expensive oils, highly touted by their makers, and you can choose from a wide variety of cutting oils, but I don't feel these are worth the price.

Start a new stone right by soaking it in kerosene until it can hold no more. In fact, I never start sharpening until the kerosene I add puddles on the surface without sinking in, and I keep adding kerosene throughout the sharpening process.

Because your plane will need sharpening so often, it's especially important that you be able to do it yourself. The goal of each sharpening is to give the knife an edge that will take off one continuous long shaving. Not only can you see and feel the difference between a dull and a sharp plane, you can also hear it. A properly sharpened hand plane almost whistles while it works; the long shaving and the whistle blend together, and the plane—at least to me—sounds happy with what it is doing.

If that sounds a little odd to you, be advised that a workman's tools develop their own personalities. Their curious little noises are a part of the communication between man and tool, a private language which, when understood, confirms the feel of harmony that can somehow link together man, tool, and wood.

When you're sharpening a plane knife, it should be held at an angle of about twenty degrees to the stone—

From left center: Electric block plane, hand power saw, belt sander, router, vibrator sander, three-eighth-inch reversible drill, sabre saw. (Photo by the author.)

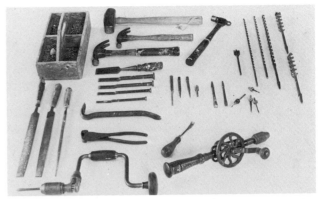

From upper left: nail tray, hammers, drills, files, chisels, nail sets, screwdriver bits, countersinks, cat's paw nail puller, nippers, bit brace, tack puller, egg beater drill. (Photo by the author.)

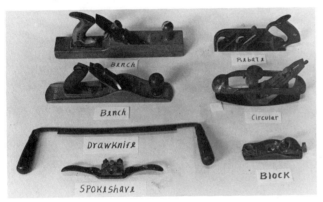

This collection of planes and knives will allow builders to cope with most any shape they encounter. (Photo by the author.)

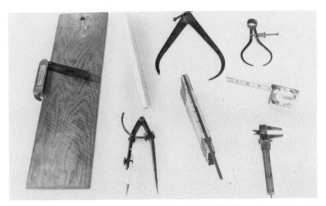

Measuring tools: bevel board with adjustable bevel, architect's scale rule, calipers, dividers, wooden six-inch extension rule, and inside/outside calipers. (Photo by the author.)

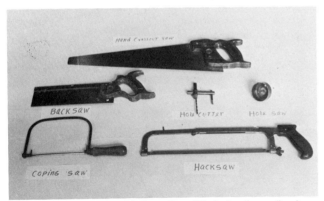

Author's hand saws and hole cutters. (Photo by the author.)

Pipe clamp and a variety of C clamps. (Photo by the author.)

just enough to make a cutting bevel surface equal to about twice the thickness of the knife.

Almost invariably, a beginner will make a circular motion as he sharpens. Such a motion is better than no motion at all, but not by much. It bends the cutting edge a little sideways, which would be readily apparent if you examined the result under a microscope. To avoid this effect, use fore-and-aft strokes or figure eights. This will produce a saw-tooth effect on the edge, which is what you want.

After a few strokes, check the top side of the knife edge with your thumb. If you don't feel a small burr, keep at it until you do. When you do feel a burr, flip the knife and make a few forward passes with the knife held flat to the stone to take the burr off, then a few more passes angled as before, and you're done.

Someone has marketed a device for holding a plane knife at just the proper angle for sharpening. Of all the gadgets devised for exploiting the uncertainties of the beginner, this one bothers me the most. Its manufacturer claims that you'll get a perfect bevel every time—and you will as long as the stone surface remains perfectly flat. But it won't; my stones testify to their hours of useful toil with a sway-backed effect. What are you supposed to do—throw the whetstone away and buy a new one every few weeks?

Granted, after repeated sharpenings, the knife bevel will develop an undesirable roundness on its underside, and that is when you take the knife to the grinding wheel and grind it back in shape—using your hand and eye to do so, and not a gadget that is incapable of making an intelligent adjustment.

When I think of all the edges that have been sharpened by old-timers without the aforementioned "aid," and with perfect results despite a well-worn stone, it bothers the hell out of me that a whole new generation of boat-builders might grow dependent on such a worse-than-useless crutch.

Moving on from sharpening a plane knife or a chisel to sharpening a hand saw, you're in a bigger league. This is not meant to be discouraging; I'm all for builders sharpening their own saws. But sharpening a saw so that it will cut freely and easily and follow a line is not something you'll learn overnight; in fact it may take as long as a year for you to get really good at it. I had the best possible teacher—my father, who filed every known type of saw commercially for decades—and it was exactly one year after I started practicing before he said, of one of my exhibits: "That's as good as I can do!"

My father never used one of those fancy file holders that are supposed to guide your file stroke; to him they were gimmicks. At one time he tinkered with an old-fashioned Foley automatic hand saw sharpener, but he never could get a job out of it to match his own freehand work. He gave the Foley to me, and soon after that my own customers started complaining, so I unbolted it from the bench and threw it over the Pleasant Beach Wharf.

Sharpening a circular saw is just as difficult, but there is an easy out on this one: buy carbon-tipped blades, which are very expensive but long-lasting. However, you can't sharpen these unless you have the required special equipment.

I still cling to file-'em-yourself blades because of the satisfaction I get from circumventing a super-tempering process that turns out everlasting teeth by machine.

I was surprised by an ad I heard on the local radio this morning, offering "New thirty-inch cordwood saws with one-and-a-half-inch arbor hole" for sale. That drops us right back into the good old days when everyone in my neighborhood burned either wood or coal. But how many people today know how to keep one of those big saws cutting? They come from the factory ready and pleasant to use, but let someone who doesn't know what he's doing file one, and it will not only fail to cut well, but will become downright dangerous. This is one good reason for keeping alive "outmoded" skills and talents.

Without going into encyclopedic detail on saw sharpening, I can give you some helpful advice. First, be sure to keep the teeth shaped exactly as the maker designed them; he had good reason for that shape. I've noticed that beginners soon file away the tooth shape, with

the result that the saw loses its ability to cut. The most common error is to file only the point of the tooth; this is easier, and for a while it works.

So when you get a new saw, lay it flat on a sheet of paper and trace around all the teeth. After you've filed the teeth a few times, check the saw against the tracing and you'll see at a glance how much, and where, you have deformed the teeth.

When you've spent years filing saws professionally, you get to know the characteristics of the various brands. In some the temper is so hard the teeth break out when you try to set them (that is, give each tooth its correct amount of offset angle from the plane of the blade); and you can't file them, either. Other blades are so soft that the teeth file too easily and won't come to a sharp point. When I see an old Disston hand saw, I use it with respect. The blades of all the Disstons I've ever filed were tempered just right. I like to think that's still true.

There's one type of saw I'd stay clear of no matter whose name is on it—a stainless-steel saw. Sure, it won't rust. It won't cut, either; the steel is too soft. There may be some reason to carry one on a boat in salt water, because when it's needed any saw beats no saw at all.

Just a light sandpapering and a wipe with an oily rag will restore a saw left outdoors overnight. If resetting the teeth is past due, a piece of paraffin ready in your pocket to slick up the blade will keep the saw cutting until it can be sharpened.

As for selecting hand-held power tools, such as power saws, electric drills, belt sanders, and the like, I look for three things: weight, balance, and my own ability to take the tool apart (or at least the assurance that my neighbor Bill Robelin 4th can take it apart) to grease and maintain it. Since I'm going to use the tool for years, price considerations come last.

Most tools will last quite well if you don't abuse them. If you're in the habit of putting a length of pipe over the handle of your Stilson wrench for more leverage, don't blame the manufacturer if the handle snaps. And don't blame him either if you keep going despite the smoke pouring off your power saw blade. You'll be blaming the wrong guy for ruining your tools.

I wouldn't consider my shop adequately equipped without a vacuum cleaner. Mine is seldom used for the floor, but it's indispensable for cleaning out dusty corners before painting a hull or clearing out any other hard-to-reach place.

And high on the nice-to-have list, if you're doing much work with fiberglass, is a shop fan. Mine is through-mounted on one wall, and in the winter, when all the doors and windows are shut tight, I breathe easier in more ways than one knowing that its blades are pulling the fumes away from me when I'm working with fiberglass.

As for lighting, I recommend the fluorescent type. It not only provides better light than incandescent lighting, it's cheaper to use.

That takes care of your eyes and your lungs; it's up to you to keep a full inventory of fingers, thumbs, and toes.

22 Paints and Finishes

The choice of paint appears to be a highly individual matter, with little or no harm done whatever you pick. So if you find something that works for you, stick with it—and with whatever special thinners, drying retardants, and the like that its maker recommends.

With all the types of paint on the market—most of which are good as far as I know—there's only one I rule out for boat work: "mill end" paint. This is the name the paint merchants give to the settlings or leavings at the bottom of the huge caldrons in which they work their magic. As I recall, it comes mainly in gray, although you can expect other colors, too. And it looks good and feels good when you're using it, but it has never stayed on for me. So until someone explains why it isn't as good as the early-run paint, I'll have to keep wondering while I keep avoiding it.

However, with all the various paints on the market, each with its own list of strange-sounding ingredients, I also wouldn't want to try mixing different brands together. Certainly the manufacturers are no help on this score, since their labels and instructions definitely convey the impression that if you wander away from their own products you're headed for disaster—perhaps even untimely death. So, while I've often sniffed at some company's special thinner and found that it has an odor suspiciously like plain old mineral spirits, I have never dared cross over.

Across the years, starting long before all the fancy formulas came out, I've grown used to oil-based paints that you can doctor yourself—such as a slug of linseed oil to make paint flow on better on a hot summer day, or a dash of Japan dryer if the air is cool and a little damp, or turpentine or mineral spirits for thinning. All these old-time additives can be had at the local hardware store without benefit of fancy names or code numbers, or borrowed from a neighbor. And while not as common as they once were, there are still plenty of oil-based paints on the market.

As Alexander Pope wrote:

Be not the first by whom the new is tried,
Nor yet the last to put the old aside.

and as far as paints are concerned, I feel somewhat justified in this cautious attitude, remembering—for example—the time when several manufacturers put out a special paint just for fiberglass that quietly faded from view when boat-builders found that it was totally unnecessary.

For reasons such as the above, I now use Woolsey Yacht paints since their labels, despite the words "acrylic formula," indicate that they include turpentine or mineral spirits along with their own numbered drying extenders and retardants. I can therefore use linseed oil and Japan dryer with these paints—with a clear conscience and no dire results either.

Another good thing about Woolsey is that they offer a neutral base undercoater—a thick-bodied paint with no color whatsoever.

For the first coat, I use three parts of this to one part of my own finish paint, which allows me to start with my chosen color and keep with it straight through to the finish coat. This means that if I happen to knock or scrape off a little paint, I will still be left with the same undercoat color.

Painting aids: Japan dryer, turpentine, putty knives, paint brush spinner for cleaning brushes, glazing putty, and paint stirrer for electric drill. (Photo by the author.)

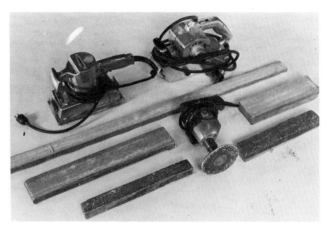

Sanding tools: power sanders, and handmade sanding blocks made especially for sanding plywood. Their long lengths bridge the soft and hard grain, and so eliminate humps and hollows. (Photo by the author.)

In fact, one very important way to produce a truly excellent finish is to pay special attention to your undercoat paints. These are rather thick paints, and should be applied thickly. Thinned just enough to permit brushing, their thickness will tend to fill any little dents or dings. When they have dried thoroughly, they can be sanded to a chalky, flat finish, with slightly darker areas indicating depressions that need more filling. You can pick up such spots by eyeballing your paint job from close to the surface; look along the length of the hull, not broad on.

Sand after each undercoat with 80- or 100-grit paper, wipe the dust off, and you're ready for the finish coats.

When painting plywood, start with two sealer coats of clear Firzite or Interlux number 1023, follow this up with two coats of undercoat paint, and top off with two finish coats. This will give a surface in which you can see your reflection. You'll think that it looks good with one coat of finish, and it does, but give it that last coat and you'll see the difference between good and excellent.

Now hear this: If you're going to paint, paint as if you meant it. None of that dip and dab business; *paint* with the paint—load your brush up and go at it. The most common fault with inexperienced painters is that they put only a little paint on the brush to begin with, and then scrape off most of that on the lip of the can. So load your brush, and slosh the paint right on.

When you're painting, use long strokes, applying plenty of pressure at first to spread the paint evenly and following through with gradually reduced pressure. For thick-bodied paints, such as undercoats, get a stirrer that will fit your electric drill; it will save you time and elbow grease.

Warm paint goes on better than cold, so if your shop is on the frigid side, warm your paint up a little.

Some people paint so slowly that every brush stroke shows. In cooler, humid weather, speed isn't too important, but when the atmosphere is hot and dry, a dollop of linseed oil and a faster brush are essential.

Another common fault of the beginner is to hit outside corners flat on with the brush. Invariably this leaves a glob of paint. If the tyro sees it run, he'll brush it right out, but will often then forget it only to see that he didn't brush it quite enough after it has sagged again and then hardened.

Lord knows I get sags, too, but having learned many coats ago that they'll form despite all my experience, I keep looking back where I've been, squinting along the skin of the hull to spot them before they harden beyond fixing. Therefore, don't put your brush away as soon as a paint job is finished; look the job over from every angle and then wait still a little longer. Otherwise you can bet that the minute you've washed your brush out and closed up the can you'll spot a run you've missed, or find that an outside corner you've hit with too much paint is just beginning to sag.

I never do any sanding between finish coats unless I see little specks of dust or a bug that has become stuck in the hardening paint. With a small bug the size of a no-see-um or even a mosquito, it's best to just leave him there and hope he croaks before he leaves his footprints all over the finish. Usually you can brush him off after the coat hardens, and his campsite will disappear with the first brush stroke of the next coat.

Don't try to use paint straight out of the can. It still amazes me that with well over a century of modern paint manufacture, no firm has come up with something better than the standard can. After trying for years to pour just a little from a full can and always ending up cursing and dumping the entire contents into a larger container, then using a little, dumping the rest back into the original container, and cleaning up the mess, I now use an 8-penny nail to drive a few little holes in the groove around the lip of the can. I then decant paint into the bottom half of a cardboard milk carton; if you jam the segment of milk carton tightly against the lip of the can, because it is flexible it will take the shape of the can and let you pour without spilling a drop. When you right your paint can, the paint that used to run down the side now drains through the little scupper holes straight into the can.

I also developed a technique for dealing with the problem of the dry layer of paint that forms atop the paint in the can: use waxed paper. Lay the can lid upside down on a sheet of the paper and trim around it with a sharp blade. You'll then have a disc that just fits the inside wall of the can. When you plop the disc on top of the remaining paint at the end of a day's work, it will settle gently down onto the surface and block out all air. Next day, when you take the paper off, you'll have only to stir, not strain, and you'll have saved a substantial amount of paint. I mass-produce these discs in required sizes and always have them handy. The only covering this won't handle is polyurethane varnish, in which the discs sink to the bottom. All my other paint cans go to the dump clean as a hound's tooth.

As for brushes, I stick with natural bristle. I never buy the nylon kind, chiefly because they're so flimsy; I also recommend using ordinary natural bristles for glue and paint jobs that will give your brushes a beating, and saving your badger-hair brushes for your top-quality efforts.

My battery of badger-hair brushes has been reduced to three calibers—one inch, one and a half inches, and two and a half inches—and it serves me well. The smaller sizes are good for corners and hard-to-reach places, and the two-and-a-half-inch width is right for long strokes both inside and outside a hull.

I used to keep my brushes in a mixture of linseed oil and turpentine. But while this kept the bristles soft enough, it made the brushes into gooey messes after they had been used with a series of different colors. Now I wash my brushes out in gasoline just as soon as I've finished painting. Gasoline is the best and fastest cleanser, and although it seems dangerous to some, I see no greater hazard in it than in the use of other solvents in my shop such as acetone and lacquer thinner. Also, there's always the great outdoors.

For final cleaning I use a pint of the International Paint Company's No. 199, a paint and varnish remover, letting the brushes soak in it overnight and then giving them a wire-brushing and a swoosh in gasoline, wrapping them in newspaper to maintain their shape, and hanging them on a nail. After one more wire-brushing before the next use, they're ready for paint again.

One final word, on touchups. If you try to cover a blemish after the paint has dried, don't expect it to blend in with the original coat; if there's a painter out there who can do a touchup job that won't show, I hope he takes time out to write about it. Until then, I'll just do the whole job over again.

Putties and fillers are closely allied to finishes, and deserve a few words here, since there's a multitude of them on the market. I don't have space to list them all, much less having had time to evaluate them. Some shrink considerably and others hardly at all; experience is your best way through this particular maze.

I've found that spot putty, which is sold in automotive-supply stores in tubes like toothpaste, works fine for small, shallow dents and hairline cracks where ordinary auto-body putty doesn't work because of its coarser consistency. Spot putty also dries fast. My only objection is that you can make only one pass with it, after which further manipulation with a putty knife will only ruffle it up. For a lot of filling, such as for knotholes in AC plywood, I like regular auto-body putty, even though it does have to be mixed with a cream hardener. Lacquer thinner can clean both types of putty off your knife; if you use it right away you'll avoid a rock-hard accumulation that must be chiseled off.

The International Paint Company makes a fine-grained trowel cement that is excellent for hairline cracks if you accept its slow-drying characteristic.

For deeper dents and in places where I'm going to varnish, I use a clear-type wood dough by Duratite. It tends to harden in the can with infrequent use, but a touch of acetone will soften it right up. I've been using the same small can of this stuff for a considerable number of years.

To cut down the number of coats needed for varnishing oak satisfactorily, I use a clear wood-paste filler of no special brand. Applied with a rag and wiped off again, it gives varnish a nice, deep glow.

Sometimes I drive a little sawdust into fresh but left-over glue and use the resulting paste for filler rather than bothering with a special mixture, particularly if the spot I'm filling is going to be painted over.

Dry powder glue mixed with fine sawdust is something else that does a pretty good job as putty, but it will tend to crack and shrink when it is used to fill in relatively deep dents, because it is a water mixture. But if the job in hand isn't too fussy, this mixture is handy and cheap, and you can always improve it by covering it over with something better later.

No-spill paint pouring: jam the milk container against the can, right up under the lip. (Photo by the author.)

An upside-down paint-can lid is used as a pattern for cutting waxed-paper discs. The size is right so the discs just clear the sides of the can and float down to the surface of the paint, effectively blocking air from the surface of the paint and preventing skimming. (Photo by the author.)

23 Sticky Subject

With the mere mention of glues and resins, I'm throwing my hat in the ring. I don't know of any more controversial subject in the boat-building field than the use, formulation, and relative safety of these compounds. And, while I rely heavily on dry-powder glue, this doesn't mean that I'm against the newer adhesives, or that I don't use them. Let's say I use them selectively.

Admittedly, I'm slower than most to commit myself to the latest "miracle" anything, so I approached the epoxies and resorcinols with caution.

When I eventually did buy some epoxy glue—the Miracle Adhesive Corporation's N.P. 428—meaning to start right in with it, I found that I couldn't even get it out of the can. Since a little heat would suffice to bring it to the consistency of molasses, I set the container on a warm spot on my stove and began stirring, hoping to bring it to brush-on consistency. Then my stirring stick began to slow down, and the next thing I knew the mix was hard as a rock and beyond recovery. The manufacturer hadn't said anything about pot life. It was a good example of the disheartening experiences that can occur when you expect the same kind of behavior from a new product as from one you're used to working with.

Anyway, because I was in the middle of building a boat, I put the epoxy aside. Several years later, I chose to try once again, this time with Chem-Tech's T-88. I picked this primarily because of its simple one-to-one mixture. The ingredients listed on the cans of the various brands of epoxy meant nothing to me, and I didn't succumb to any claims of usability in freezing weather with wood of a high moisture content, or ability to harden under water, as I avoid all these conditions in my building style. However, I found some of T-88's qualities much to my liking. I tested its flexibility by anchoring a flapping shoe sole with it, and I'm still wearing the shoes.

I'm happy with T-88 for gluing surfaces together on the flat, such as in laminating a rudder or a leeboard; it is also great for gluing spars. But I'm not all that smitten with its performance in vertical joints—like all the epoxies I've seen so far, even though it's thick enough to require a putty knife rather than a brush for application, it tends to run out of such joints like water. Some builders get around this problem by adding one of the various fillers or powders to stiffen the glues up; without such additives they'd have a tough time living up to their proclaimed gap-filling capability.

Impressive specs are well and good, but I know no boat-builders who work under the laboratory conditions manufacturers apparently enjoy. I have no idea what force, in terms of pounds per square inch, I'm applying when I clamp two boards together, but only that, if I use epoxy resin sparingly and drag it out with a putty knife, then the right clamp pressure is what will squeeze the mix out at the edges. As for testing joint sheer re-sistance, trying to break the joint over your knee is not a bad way to go.

I could also wish for a bit more honesty in advertising claims. I'm particularly bothered by the free-and-easy tossing around of the word "penetration" as applied to epoxy resins. Boat building sage John Gardner took up the cudgels on this score in an article in *National Fisherman* (Camden, Me.: 1980), in which he noted that all epoxies are deficient in four respects: (1) they do not penetrate wood in any meaningful sense; (2) they are heavy; (3) they are expensive; (4) there is the possibility of serious long-term health hazard for those who work with them on a regular basis over extended periods.

As for penetration, I once watched master builder Merrill Young perched on top of the stem of a forty-footer he was building, pouring linseed oil into a funnel stuck in a hole bored in the stem head. You could see oil oozing out of the sides of the stem clear down to the forefoot. That's penetration.

And thanks to John Gardner's words of warning, I've quit using acetone to wash my hands free of epoxy or polyester resins, knowing that acetone dissolves fatty tissue and drives resins under the skin. I'm also more careful with fumes and dust.

I'll continue to use epoxy resins because they'll do jobs that no other adhesives I've used can handle. For taping a chine or laminating wood, I doubt if you can beat epoxy. But I have no desire to use it for laying up a cold-molded hull out of strips of wood all day; building boats is a pleasant occupation and I want to be around as long as I can to enjoy it to the fullest. As for sanding epoxy resins, I find them worse than the polyesters because of slow curing and sandpaper fill-up, which often destroys the usefulness of a sheet of paper after just one pass. Chem-Tech recommends washing epoxied surface before sanding it, but I've never tried this.

Resorcinol glues? I've used a lot of this two-part mix of beet-colored resin and powder catalyst, and I still do. The glue stays where you put it in a vertical joint, with never a drip. When it is almost used up and has begun to thicken, the remainder makes a good putty that will stay in a joint without benefit of filler.

The labels of resorcinol-glue cans carry precise and helpful information on mixing, specifying the hardening time at recommended temperatures. Even if you can't match your shop temperature to the specs, you can still use the glue. Just expect to wait a little longer; as long as the mixture is in the right proportions, it will eventually harden up.

I have only two reservations about resorcinol glue: it lacks the flexibility of epoxies, and it will show through light-toned paints even when cleaned off as best you can manage and with four coats of paint on top of sealer. The color keeps coming through, just like creosote.

The dry-powder glue developed around the mid-1940s was very likely the most widely used adhesive until the exotics came on the market. It is both cheap and easy to use, and although the container directions suggest you not use it in temperatures below seventy degrees, I know from experience that you can depend on it at considerably below that.

For the small boats we're talking about, which are never subjected to the most extreme strains, I see no reason to stop using dry-powder glue, especially when bonding soft wood to soft wood. There is never a problem as long as the mixture has been brought to the heavy-cream consistency called for in the directions.

You're better off mixing a dry glue with cold water. When added a little at a time, this makes a nice creamy mixture with no fuss. Hot water makes lumps, which call for strenuous stirring.

I apply this glue with a brush and wash out the bristles with the hottest water my shop stove can produce, right after every application. I've lost a good many brushes by being lax about this; with the prices tagged on even cheap brushes today, I'm now careful to keep

them clean and flexible. Tongue depressors make great glue spreaders, too, but are slower.

Although the dry-glue maker says nothing about failure-proof joints, I've yet to see any disturbing evidence of this problem. The only failure I've witnessed was with my own skiff, which happened when another fisherman threw his boat down on top of it. They weren't a nesting fit, so I found mine with the sides hanging off the stem next morning when I went down to go aboard.

With epoxy and resorcinols costing as much as forty dollars a gallon at the time of this writing, and ten pounds of dry powder going for ten or twelve bucks, I'll be using more of the latter. And as for the matter of health, I prefer to build boats, not my tombstone, in my shop.

One last thing about the glue you use: whatever it is, someone will be ready and eager to tell you it's the wrong kind. You can be sure that the Great Glue Controversy will continue, and you can hope that if it accomplishes nothing else, it will subdue exaggerated advertising claims.

24 Spars

If you were playing a word-association game and someone tossed out the cue word "spar," the chances are ten to one that any expert in nautical niceties would flash out "Sitka spruce!" with the speed of a knee-joint responding to a rubber hammer.

Forget it; there is no need for a big cash outlay and the hunting down of semi-precious woods if you're just thinking of masts, booms, or sprits that will spread your sails efficiently.

I sometimes think that spar-making has been elevated to the status of mystery. Few boat-building books offer much real help on the subject. Howard Chapelle, in his *Boatbuilding*, has described a detailed procedure, but it's not applicable to the size of boat we're talking about building.

I'm convinced that you can't beat a natural-grown tree for a small mast, because you don't cut and disturb the grain pattern while shaping it. But few of us have access to suitable trees, so if you're not going to be fussy, you can probably find the wood you want in your local lumberyard. The lowly two-by-four, selected for reasonably good grain, will work perfectly well, even though it may be loaded with small, tight knots (avoid stock with the big, black ones). Compared to anything else, the price of two-by-fours is still right and likely to remain so as long as houses are built competitively.

When I built the prototype of Phil Bolger's folding

schooner—a thirty-one-foot craft whose hull was hinged in the middle to adapt it for trailering—I used two-by-fours for the masts. Each mast was made up of two sixteen-foot lengths taken right off the lumberyard pile, glued together back-to-back, and worked into the round. Made like this they're perfectly satisfactory if you're careful to do your laminating with the grains of the two pieces opposed.

Courage is a useful asset in mast-making. I once talked to a man who had begun as an apprentice under old J. Arthur Stevens of Goudy and Stevens in East Boothbay, Maine: "My first day on the job, he asked me if I had ever made a mast. I said 'No,'" the man recalled. " 'You're going to make one today,' he told me, and by God when the quitting whistle blew I had."

Rounding a mast by hand is a tough job if you really try to keep the spar perfectly round in cross-section throughout. I wonder if a set of calipers tried here and there on the entire length of some of the products of the old masters might show a little less than perfect roundness, undetectable at a casual glance. Of course, the bigger masts never had to turn in a partner anyway; the mast hole had plenty of leeway and the stick was firmly wedged to the proper rake.

Before we start any rounding, let's get those two lengths of two-by-four firmly glued together. And—as I learned the hard way—don't just lay the pieces across a couple of sawhorses. If you do, you'll be shocked when you get the last clamp on them and look back to check for straightness. The weight of the clamps will warp the lamination. You must place the clamps close together, spaced about nine or ten inches apart at the most. With no support and a fast-setting glue, you can expect a permanently bent spar.

The best procedure is to glue the assembly right on the floor, if it's level, and to use shims if it's not. Lay down waxed paper first, to keep the floor free of glue. Lacking floor space, snap a chalk line along the two-by-four studs in your shop wall and nail a support for the spar to each stud.

My second hard-earned lesson came when I was eight-siding a spar that already had the proper taper, and took the same amount of wood off the truck, or top of the mast, as I did off the larger butt. To illustrate the problem I was dealing (unsuccessfully) with, and the proper approach, consider one of the masts for the Bolger folding schooner I mentioned. By specification, it must be round with a three-inch diameter for about three-quarters of its length, and must then taper to one and a half inches at the truck.

With the lamination completed, begin by drawing diagonals from corner to corner across the butt. With their intersection as the center, swing a three-inch circle with a compass. Do the same at the other end, with a one-and-one-half-inch diameter circle drawn in the center of the truck end. Start the taper by drawing a center-line along the laminated stick and measuring widths out from that. Sweep in the curve with a batten, and saw the taper. Flip the spar over, and repeat on the other side. Then, with your table saw set at forty-five degrees take off the corners as close as possible to the three-inch circle drawn on the butt. Where the taper starts, decrease the depth of the cut from there to the masthead, or truck.

Eight-siding a mast stick with your table saw or hand power saw is difficult enough; I don't recommend using these tools for sixteen-siding, which is pretty close to round. With sixteen corners to trim, it's easy to find yourself planing where you shouldn't. I've made a spar-plane from a reshaped wooden smooth plane. It does a good job, but even so I admit I've made very few round spars so far that I'm totally happy with.

For a small mast that must rotate in its partner and still fit closely at this location—as in the case of the Thomaston Galley—I'm very fussy about achieving a round section right at that point; but if the rest of the mast is a little out of round I don't lose any sleep. I don't put any taper in the Galley's two-inch mast, but I do taper the one-and-a-half-inch sprit slightly at each end.

Obviously, a solid square-section spar is the easiest to make, although the grain must be carefully inspected for signs of gross irregularities and potentially weakening knots. Lacking the opposed grain of a lamination, such a spar is apt to go out of straight when a saw cut releases the inner stress of the grain, and since you can do nothing about it, if your mast should take such a bend, just set the concave side facing forward and forget it.

Another type of mast—a light, hollow box spar—is simple enough in design and its components are easy to make, but with four edges to glue and hold in place while you're clamping the four longitudinals, the building process can be a very bothersome one. If you choose to build this type of mast, you must beef it up at the partner and where any fittings are to be installed by gluing in solid wood-block inserts at these points.

While we're on the subject of spars, it might be well to elaborate on the design of the sprit and the mast fittings of the Thomaston Galley, which are none too explicit on the designer's plans.

As the drawings indicate, the function of the sprit is to raise and extend the peak of the quadrilateral sail, much as the gaff does in more conventional rigs. This spar has a quarter-inch slot cut into each end; the slot at the top of the sprit engages a "pigtail" in the peak of the sail—either an eyesplice or a short line with a "stopper" knot at its end—and the slot at the lower end of the sprit receives a line called the snotter, also with a stopper knot on one end, which serves to brace up and hold the sprit to keep the peak in an elevated position. The mast has two cleats mounted on it. Made fast to one of these is the sling, a short line of about nine inches which has a thimble, or metal eye, spliced into its free end. The unknotted end of the snotter runs through the thimble to gain the purchase needed to shove the sprit against the peak of the sail, much as a halyard renders through a block, or pulley, to hoist an ordinary sail. When the sail has been firmly snugged up, the free end of the snotter is made fast to the other cleat on the mast. Then the sailor, sheet in hand, can retire to the glory seat and take the tiller.

25 Scarphing Plywood

The scarphing of timbers or grain planks—joining two lengths end-to-end without a butt block—is well covered by many manuals, but this is not extended to include plywood. True, I have read quite a few descriptions of how to scarph plywood using a hand plane, all pretty much in agreement on the proper length of the joint (twelve times the thickness of the sheet), and all accompanied by neat drawings, but I have never seen a photograph of a scarphed plywood joint. In fact, I never saw one of these joints until I made my own. So if the art of scarphing plywood scares the pants off you, join the club! It took several false starts, but ultimately the dragon didn't turn out to be so very fierce.

In the end I conned myself into doing it. I had picked up a bargain of thirty-two fourteen-foot-long sheets of five-sixteenths-inch Triple-A marine grade plywood when my chief need was for sixteen-foot lengths. There was nothing wrong with the five-sixteenths-inch thickness (in fact, I wish the plywood companies would offer that size all the time); the original purchaser had planned to build a fleet of small V-bottom runabouts with it. But after he dropped from view the pile had gathered dust in the Rockland Boat Shop for several years. When Sulo Gronos offered it to me at a price of twenty cents a foot as against the then-going rate of forty to fifty cents, I lugged it home.

I began my scarphing with the universally recommended hand plane, and got nowhere. Next I tried using a hand power saw set to the appropriate bevel on a jury-rig arrangement, and still went nowhere. Convinced that the desired perfection could never be achieved with hand-working methods, I concocted a series of scarphing techniques using jigs in every way possible.

I finally identified the heart of the problem: An everyday, garden-variety mental block. So I took up my combination square and marked off three and a half inches on each of the ends to establish the approximately twelve-to-one taper ratio, clamped an end down with a dead-flat piece of three-eighths-inch aluminum to support the feather edge I was aiming for, and cut the bevel with my electric hand-block plane.

That feather edge on both pieces is vital; otherwise, when you put them together and clamp down, applying pressure, they will slip endwise even if the edges are a mere sixteenth of an inch thick.

I took off all the wood I dared, keeping a close eye on the veneers for straightness, and finished the taper with an electric belt sander using 60-grit paper. During this process I kept checking the joint for straightness with the back of my handsaw.

Next, I mated the two tapers for accuracy of fit. If the veneers that run with the direction of cutting seem too smooth, they can be roughened up a little with a wood rasp or whatever. When I was making up trial panels for the across-the-knee break test, I made up some smooth and some roughened joints, and couldn't detect any strength difference. Even so, I still use the roughening process.

With long, hard-to-handle sections of a boat, such as the bottom panels for the Galley and the side panels for the Gloucester light dory, I see no alternative to making the joint anyplace you have room enough to stretch out your long piece of plywood. For sections short enough to fit on your table saw, however, that's the tool with which to make the taper, or at least take off a good part of it.

If this process seems too wearisome to you, you might try the scarphing attachment sold by Gougeon Brothers, of Bay City, Michigan, which can be used with most hand-held circular saws. The eight-to-one taper this device produces, though shorter than the usual twelve-to-one taper, has nothing wrong with it so far as I can see, especially if you can place your joint over a frame. But for the joints I use such as those in the Galley and the dory, where the gunwale and chine provide the only backing, I'll stick with the longer, hand-made taper. Although the Gougeon sales literature shows a real scarph joint in the making, and it looks good, for my purposes I'd feather the edge more than the Gougeon pictures show. Plywood has a tendency to buckle, and it looks to me as if a wiggle or a waver in the sawing process could put the blade where it has no business being unless the edge is somehow supported in a straight line.

Most treatises on scarphing plywood recommend using

Electric hand block plane makes short work of cutting taper. (Photo by the author.)

The taper is then sanded to a knife edge with an electric belt sander using 60-grit paper. (Photo by the author.)

nails to keep the joint from slipping. Don't. If your tapers aren't accurate, no nails are going to keep them from slipping; if they are accurate, you won't need nails. Yet there is the possibility of some slippage when you apply pressure, so it is best to leave a little extra wood all around. When I made up my sixteen-foot panels, I left a half-inch all around, then put my side pattern on again later, to check my dimensions before I made a final cut.

To ensure proper alignment, strike a straight line through the joint, at a right angle to it, for a distance of three to four feet, and watch this line for sidewise misalignment when you put the squeeze on the joint.

To get absolutely even pressure, clamp the joint sandwich style when you glue it up, using boards at least three-quarters of an inch thick, wide enough and long enough to span the joint. Put waxed paper on both sides of the joint and a board on each side, then use clamps that are deep enough to clamp the whole thing down to a sawhorse.

When gluing a scarphed joint I use resorcinol—it's good enough for the plywood companies—and mix it

right to the letter of the instructions, even regulating my shop temperature. When you apply the glue, it will sink into the end grain of the plywood veneers but not into the flat surface of the wood. Before you close the joint permanently, leave it open for a few minutes; if it looks as if the end grain has absorbed too much glue, add another dash or two. At seventy degrees, you won't have long to wait for the joint to cure. Anything lower than that will take a little longer. Keep the temperature steady throughout the curing process if you can.

Take up on both clamps as evenly as you can, and keep your eye on that match-up line for misalignment. A few nails on either side of the joint might help, but I don't use them.

Next day when the joint is thoroughly cured, remove the excess glue with your belt sander, finish with a vibrator sander, and you'll have a joint to be proud of.

But don't just assume the joint is good enough. Make a few test panels first, and if, when you break them across your knee, the joint splinters out instead of letting go straight across, you can trust your work in any boat you build.

The joint is tested for straightness with the back of my hand saw. (Photo by the author.)

The two tapers are glued and clamped together; waxed paper on both sides of the joint prevents the excess glue from sticking the whole assembly together while the glue is drying. (Photo by the author.)

26 A Suit of Glass Armor

"Burn her? like hell I will!"

That was my response to the suggestion made by the insurance adjustor who viewed the remains of my stone-walled lobster boat. He wasn't alone; I had plenty of friends who had already said the same thing.

I could hardly blame them. Split from stemhead to keel, the boat looked like prime fodder for a bonfire. In fact, my own immediate reaction had been that I might as well burn her. It took a while for my eye to probe beyond the shambles and see that her thin skin of a single layer of glass cloth was still intact, and that if I could coax the hood ends of her planks back into the stem rabbet, there was a good chance that I could make her as tight as a jug again.

The immediate aim of glassing an old boat is to gain a tight boat, and I had glassed her a year or two before the disaster because she was too loose here and there to hold caulking any more, and too old to make retimbering and refastening worthwhile.

I had given her only one layer, which sufficed perfectly well for quite a while. It had minor drawbacks, such as cracks that needed patching before each spring relaunching, and small bubbles that formed as she alternately swelled and shrank from her seasons in the water and out.

But when you glass an old boat, you also gain a faster boat; I couldn't believe the extra knots that lobster boat made with her new skin. Her copper-painted wooden bottom had always seemed smooth to me, but maybe all those seams had produced enough skin friction to slow her down. After fiberglassing, the ease with which she slipped through the water was itself justification for the job. And in the end it had even saved her life.

So let's assume that you are going to give an old painted wooden hull of your own a suit of glass armor.

Dry the hull thoroughly first, then take its finish down to bare wood with a high-speed disc sander. Use the heavy-duty type that auto-body repairmen favor, with a very coarse disc that looks as though rocks were stuck

into the paper like raisins. I don't remember the brand name of the one I borrowed, but it was no toy—it took everything in its path, including nail and bolt heads. With a masticator like this, wear a face mask and keep the sander moving. Linger on one spot even briefly, and

Hood ends of the planks were coaxed back into the stem rabbet, and a piece of damaged plank has been replaced. A batten tacked on to the face of the stem provides a guide for restoring its shape. Fiberglass filler putty fills the gap between the damaged area and the batten. (Photo by the author.)

Stem is reglassed and sanded. (Photo by the author.)

Author's son Timothy with busted boat (now twenty-five years old). With the help of one layer of fiberglass, she's still fishing. (Photo by the author.)

97

With the stem finished and waterline restruck, she's watertight again and ready for work. (Photo by the author.)

you'll dig a groove you'll have to fill in later.

Disc sanding will leave just the rough surface you want for the best glass adhesion; don't smooth it. Round off all the corners by at least three-eighths of an inch. Next, fill in all the outside cracks in the bare hull with auto-body putty or something similar that doesn't have an oil base. If the inside planking seams show wide and deep, don't fill them with anything that will set up hard. The hull is going to grow with moisture when the boat goes back into the water, even after fiberglassing, and the skin will stretch and cause wrinkles when it dries again.

I saw no need for digging out all the putty in the outside seams, even though it was oil-based; I just took care to fill them with the auto-body putty so that the resin wouldn't soak through the cloth to the inside of the boat.

With the sanding done and the dust cleaned off, check the hull for oily spots on the planking and wash off any that you find with lacquer thinner or anything else that will cut the grease, and you're ready to glass.

Don't brood about any special techniques when it comes to the size of the cloth pieces you put on. A single layer isn't going to inject structural strength into the hull anyway, so cut and match the cloth where you want. But the bigger the pieces and the fewer the seams, the better the job will look and probably be.

You'll be amazed to see what you can do with the resin-wetted cloth. Places where you think you'll have to do some cutting of unwanted puckers will simply take care of themselves when you stretch out a properly saturated piece of cloth. Don't take my word for it, do it; you'll see.

Fiberglass cloth comes in rolls thirty-eight, forty-four, and sixty inches wide, and in various weights. I'd choose

the ten-ounce weight for the kind of work we're talking about. All three of the rolls I inquired about came in this weight.

Some builders put resin on the bare wood first, let it get tacky, and then slap the cloth on. I usually put the cloth on dry, pouring the resin with the cloth in place on the wood. Only on a vertical surface do I apply resin to the wood first and press the cloth into it.

Also, when you're working with a large piece of cloth, start with your resin right in the middle of the piece. Mix up only about a pint of resin at a time, and work from the center outward, in ever widening swaths, so you don't entrap any air.

With your boat upside down, measure the distance amidships from sheer to keel, and take the overall length. Let's say you're working on a round-bottom boat sixteen feet long, with five feet from sheer to keel, and a transom width of five feet. I'd ask the clerk to whack off seventeen yards of thirty-eight-inch cloth for the job. The choice of width should be the same whether you plan to lap over the keel directly or first lay a strip over the keel along the whole length of the boat and then lap over onto that.

I've done it both ways, and I've found the job is far more difficult if you use a piece of cloth wide enough to go from one sheer, over the keel and down to the planking on the other side. This method will produce bubbles right alongside the keel. You might get the cloth well saturated and laid just right over the keel, but because you've stretched the cloth somewhere else, you will look back and discover an air pocket where the keel and planking meet. Once started this way, there's nothing you can do but keep working at it until you finally get the mess straightened out.

It's far easier to take a strip of cloth about a foot wide, lay it the length of the keel, and start pouring the resin right on the keel; stick the strip of cloth in place and then work down the sides of the keel and onto the planking, getting rid of air bubbles as you go.

Next, take a piece of cloth large enough to cover the transom and lap over onto the bottom by some four or five inches. With that wetted down in place, it's time for the big pieces of cloth, one to each side of the keel, that mate with the keel strip and the transom overlap.

I don't try to gain a good fit along the under edge of the gunwale until the cloth is completely wetted out and has started to get tacky; then I roll the resin as close as I can come to the gunwale, let it set up a bit, and trim off the excess with a sharp knife.

Finally, I work the edge down with a paint brush filled with a load of resin.

Anywhere there is a lap, there will be a bulge unless you first fair off the edge of the first layer of cloth. (There is a school of thought that favors butting the edges instead of lapping; that may be all right if you're applying more than one layer of cloth, but even then I don't subscribe to it.)

By using plain layup resin—not the store-bought kind that contains wax—you can do the keel area first, then let it dry enough to feather the edges before the next layer, and follow the same procedure for the transom lap. (As I explained earlier, work done with the wax kind can't be interrupted and then resumed unless sanding is done between coats.) The keel should be built up of at least three or four layers of cloth. Even that is none too thick, but will suffice if you don't plan to land on the beach very often.

Fiberglass is good for gaining watertightness, but—as mentioned earlier—is no substitute for structural strength. If any of your bent frames are rotted or cracked, they should be replaced or sistered before glassing. If you can stomach working with matting instead of cloth, you'll gain strength in the covering, but you'll increase both the weight of your boat and the cost of the glassing job.

I see no reason why the beginner shouldn't undertake fiberglassing the average round-bottom boat or canoe with confidence. The only hull I'd shy away from is a lapstrake hull; one look at all those laps, each just waiting to entrap air, and I have a fiberglass nightmare.

Fiberglass, as a strengthening adjunct, is the material that makes building plywood boats a sensible proposition, and it can perform a valuable service in extending the life of an aging wooden hull. Building boats of it is another matter. All things considered, I'd prefer to pass down to my grandchildren the heritage of woodworking skill rather than artistry with a brush and a bucket.

27 Start Small

Some years back, I sold a set of Gloucester light dory plans to a highly skilled machinist, along with a stick of good oak for the stem. Months later I asked him how he was coming along. The piece of oak, he reported, was safely tucked away in his bedroom closet.

That machinist is far from being a unique case; I've met plenty of cabinetmakers who do such exacting work that it scares *me*, yet some bugaboo stands between them and a boat they would truly like to build. There are many fields that nurture experts in close fitting. If I ever bet on a spiling contest between a linoleum layer and a boat-builder, I know where I'll put my dough.

What is there about building a boat that seems to scare many an accomplished craftsman? People who seem ideally suited to produce a well-made boat just don't do it. It could be that they're stymied by a degree of perfectionism that's carried to a point at which they can't bear to start manhandling large pieces of wood in what is essentially a much less demanding process than they're accustomed to.

To the competent craftsman who turns craven when faced with a set of boat plans—and the less-than-competent tool user who is convinced that any pile of nice wood to which he takes edged tools will inevitably be reduced to a pile of scrap—I say: *start with a model.*

If you've followed my suggestion of designing a boat by making a lift model, you have probably gained two things: a full grasp of the problems and solutions involved in shaping a boat, and a sound understanding of the process by which the idea of a boat becomes a boat.

When you make a model of a chine boat like the Gloucester dory or the Thomaston Galley, you come much closer to the actual building process. Using your scale rule you can make a miniature jig for the hull, using plywood, and you can saw out the sides, bottom, and transom from thin strips of ordinary white pine or cedar on your table saw. In gluing the pieces together you carry out essentially the same operations as in building a full-size hull. I can't think of a better spare-time winter project. And when it's finished, you will have something quite nice to have around.

You will also be drawn, I suspect, into that special appreciation of a hull that comes from seeing it in the round—and not just seeing it, but actually turning it in your hands. There is a kind of magic in the miniature. You may have read every section of *Gulliver's Travels*, a rather long book with a variety of journeys to strange places, but I'll bet that when you think of Gulliver it is the citizens of Lilliput you see—those perfect minuscule human beings with all their fascinating tools, possessions, structures, and weapons just like ours—only smaller. Call it the fascination of perspective.

I started making models of the boats for which I sell plans or finished hulls so that I would have something in my shop to show to customers, something that wasn't buried under a ton of snow in my yard. But now the models have moved into my living room and my den, and I can look at them with pleasure every day.

I am thinking of my friend Jay Hanna of Rockport, Maine—wood carver, design engineer, fabricator of industrial models—who is recognized the world over for his marine miniatures. He has planked up ship models using nails he has made himself, and has cast his own fittings meticulously scaled down from actual size. But the models are so fine that they end up in museum collections; I get to keep mine.

So don't carry model-making too far; stay within the bounds of the practical, and you'll find it much easier to make your first saw cut in that good boat-building wood.

28 A Boat Owner's Guide to a Good Night's Sleep

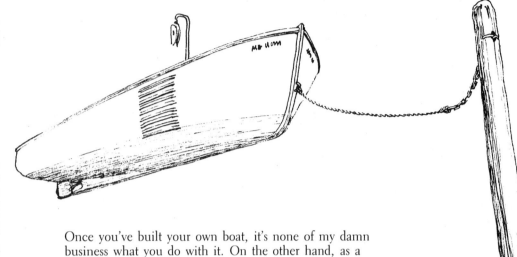

Once you've built your own boat, it's none of my damn business what you do with it. On the other hand, as a lifetime fisherman, boat-builder, and boat owner—and consequently a veteran worrier about the well-being of a considerable number of craft of various types—I feel obliged to pass along a foolproof prescription for peace of mind.

I'm talking about a kind of mooring that has proved itself drag-free in virtually all tides and weathers for many a decade, and probably for centuries. Fishermen who must moor in exposed waters—as I did for ten years off a dot of an island called Metinic—bet their boats on it, every night. So can you.

It's known as a pole mooring, and in my locale we've added a refinement called the Devil's Claw. The pole acts as a shock absorber. Its lower end is chained to whatever you're relying on to make you fast to the bottom. Its upper end carries about eight inches of chain when you're hooked on to it; in fact, this short chain is part of your painter. The Devil's Claw is a device that links your boat securely to both these chains.

Rigged like this, your boat never pulls directly against the dead weight of the mooring, even when a building sea does its damnedest to make it do so. Two hurricanes have gone to work on my mooring rig, with nothing to show for their pains but a boatful of water.

For the mooring, I suggest a four- or five-hundred-pound chunk of granite. As an alternative—or a stopgap while you're searching for the stone—I recommend an old engine block. Over a soft bottom you could use a large self-burying mushroom anchor of, say, seventy-five pounds or so. Salt water has a taste for nibbling at concrete, so be advised to rule out that undeservedly popular make-weight from the start—unless, that is, you're an expert mixer of concrete and know exactly what you're doing when you mix up a batch for your mooring.

The log mooring.

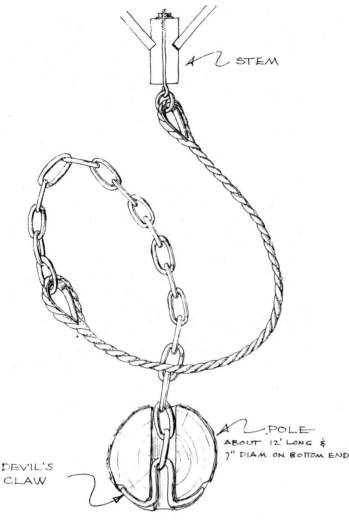

A⌐⌐ STEM

DEVIL'S
CLAW

A⌐⌐ POLE
ABOUT 12' LONG &
7" DIAM ON BOTTOM END

The Devil's Claw.

For tying up a small, light craft of fifteen to twenty feet to the pole mooring, you should have at least three-eighths-inch chain. Get black iron; galvanized won't last one bit longer, if as long. If you're using an engine block, don't fasten the chain around the crankshaft—sooner or later its bolts will give up. Instead, remove a piston and lead the chain through the empty bore. Cut through the end link and return the chain to form a loop just large enough to lead the other end through. The cut link will have to be spot welded, or—and much better—fitted with a ring made up by your local blacksmith, if you have one. The ring lets you remove the chain without tools, and if your mooring is set in clear, shallow water and you can reach it with a gaff, you can switch chains without taking the mooring ashore.

If you're securing the chain to a granite block, you'll need a staple—a large U-shape with legs at least three-quarters of an inch in diameter and long enough to penetrate the granite block and protrude through its other side. This means drilling holes through the block. You can have this done in jig time if you can arrange to have a pneumatic drill come to your rock, or vice versa. I recommend you do it yourself.

Any rock drill will work. Use a light maul, three to four pounds in weight. Once you get the hole started, keep turning the drill with every whack. Pour in a little water from time to time to carry away the dust, and wrap a rag around the work to keep from getting splattered. You can figure on a half to three-quarters of an hour of pounding for each hole in a slab eight or nine inches thick. It's not all that tough to do, and it's a great way to work out your aggressions. Once the holes are cut and the chain is linked into the bight of the staple, use a five-pound maul or better to bend the protruding staple ends over.

Spruce, fir, or cedar will do nicely for the pole. Cut it ten to twelve feet long from a trunk that will give you a butt diameter of seven to eight inches, and a diameter of five or six inches at the small end. Leave the bark on to slow down water absorption. Cut two poles so you can switch them at the end of a season and always have one drying. Together, the length of the pole and the depth of the water will determine the minimum length of your chain: it must be long enough for you to pull the pole up and get at the bottom end, at least at low tide. The longer the chain, the better the holding power, but the amount of room your boat has to swing in is the limiting factor.

Now for the Devil's Claw. As drawn, it's a simple loop of wrought iron with the open ends bent over at a slightly acute angle. You'll need two of these, one for each end of the pole. Drill holes for these through the pole, about eight inches from each end; they must be large enough for the chains to pass through, and to accept the loops of the Devil's Claws. Cut and gouge two grooves alongside each hole, into which the prongs can haul back when you put a strain on the rig.

Use three-quarter-inch line for the painter. Splice it with a thimble to your stem fitting at one end, and similarly with another thimble through the end link of the eight-inch length of chain at the other.

You now have the simplest tie-up ever. You don't even have to work from the bow to use it. Bring your boat alongside the pole, Devil's Claw ready in one hand and the chain end of the painter in the other. Lead the chain through the hole in the end of the pole, thread the claw into the end link, and haul back. You're hooked. When you're getting underway from the mooring, just bat the claw backward and take it aboard. If you're afraid of losing it, make up an extra claw or two and keep them handy aboard. That's what all we Devil's Claw addicts do.

If it should occur to you to substitute some type of quick-release shackle for the claw, deep-six the thought. With the two claws you're free of shackles, welds, bolts, and any other vulnerable link in the chain of your mooring. Only the chain itself requires occasional inspection, and handling the claw as frequently as you will, you'll note any wear from its riding on the chain in plenty of time to replace it with a new one.

There's only one monkey wrench that can be thrown into this simple piece of machinery. If the painter should ever get below the end of the pole, it will saw itself in two on the chain. No problem: just keep your painter too short to duck under the pole's lower end.

And there you are. To borrow from Mark Twain, you will now share the calm confidence of a Christian with five aces.

If sometime in the future you decide that you would like to relocate your mooring, don't be dismayed by the magnitude of the task. Given the use of a sixteen-foot boat of the type discussed in the first section of this book, moving a four- or five-hundred-pound rock doesn't even qualify as a chore.

At dead low water, go forward and take aboard all the chain you can over the bow, straightening out any twists as you bring it in. When the chain is straight up and down, make it fast, through one of the links, to the eye-bolt or bow eye. A couple of turns of nylon pot warp will do the job nicely.

Then go aft and start your motor. Just the shifting of your weight from up forward, where it put the bow down and gave you a deeper bite on the chain, to aft in the stern sheets where it levers the bow up, will be enough to get the mooring off the bottom, and the power of the motor will help break it out. If there is shallower water or some obstruction on the bottom between you and your new location, let the lift of the incoming tide provide the clearance you need. You'll find that with the weight hanging from the bow and the stern left free to swing, steering will be a lead- pipe cinch.

Before you drop your mooring again, make absolutely certain that the chain is free to run overboard—when that rock heads for the bottom you don't want anything or anybody in the way. Moreover, do *not* attempt to untie the knot that secures the rig to the boat; you can lose fingers that way. Cut the line with a good sharp knife, and stand well clear when you let her go.

To lift a larger rock, all the way up to a ton or two, a couple of dories side by side with a stout pole lashed across them to take the strain will carry it off like nothing at all.

I'll spare you the usual homilies on ground tackle in general; they're available from all sides. But a word on what might be termed the Gunkholer's Delight: This is a five-pound mushroom anchor, or for that matter any handy rock you can make a line fast to when you're tempted to land and explore. After you've run up on the beach, balance the mushroom or whatever on the transom, get out of your boat, and give her a steady shove out. When she's out far enough so she won't be left high and dry by the tide, jerk the painter to topple the anchor off. Then tie up to the nearest tree, and you'll be able to put out to sea again without having to drag your craft through a dozen yards or so of tidal mud or sharp rocks.

29 Signing Off

Talking with Jay Hanna one day, I wondered aloud if there was any legitimate place for another how-to book in the boat-building field. There are so many, I said, how could I justify writing one more?

Jay, with a couple of volumes of his own on wood-carving under his belt and a library crammed with the works of others, disagreed: "If every time a new book comes out dealing with a subject that interests me I learn at least one thing I never knew before, the book was worth writing."

But there's something beyond that.

Among the men who ply the various trades, I have observed that the ones who work with boats—designers, builders, and users—are usually happier than most oth-ers, and of these, the very happiest in my opinion are boat-builders who use edged tools and work in wood. Such work makes demands on, and seems therefore to satisfy, the whole man—hand, eye, ear, brain, and heart.

Admittedly, I'm prejudiced. Not everyone is a dedicated hard-core boat-building nut. But I think all of us, from the whittled-chip-in-the-puddle days on, have some streak in our nature that is drawn to the making and using of boats. Therefore any development of that ingredient can't help but add to the development of the whole person.

So I hope that this book has had something to say to that part of your conglomerate psyche.

GLOSSARY

ABAFT: toward the stern of a boat; the mast is abaft the stem.

AMIDSHIPS: roughly, the central area of a boat's hull, halfway between the bow and the stern; as an adjective, midship.

ATHWARTSHIPS: running across a hull, at right angles to its keel; as an adjective, thwartship.

BASELINE: a line drawn on boat plans, running the length of the hull, usually parallel to the waterline or the keel, from which all vertical measurements are taken in lofting the lines of a hull.

BATTEN: a thin, flat strip of wood used to assist in drawing a fair curve by springing it along a series of reference points.

BEVEL: an angular cut, expressed in degrees, that permits wood-to-wood contact between members of a boat's hull.

BILGE: that portion of a boat's bottom between the keel and the waterline.

BREASTHOOK: a transverse structural member between the uppermost planks of a hull near the stem.

BUNG: a disc of wood used to plug the recess of a countersink and thus cover the head of a fastening to maintain a flush surface.

BUTT: to meet and join end-to-end or edge-to-edge. A butt joint is used to extend a short piece of planking, or a panel, to the full length of a hull or any shorter required distance. Of a mast, its lower end.

BUTT BLOCK: a short piece of wood used to lap over and strengthen a butt joint on the inside surface of the hull.

BUTTOCK: an imaginary vertical slice through a boat's hull, cut lengthwise and parallel to the centerline. Buttock lines are sometimes plotted on boat plans to provide additional reference points for lofting.

CARVEL PLANKING: smooth-seamed planking, formed by fastening planks edge-to-edge along the hull without overlapping.

CAULKING: fibrous material such as cotton, which is driven into the seams of a hull to seal them watertight and then covered over with a puttylike compound.

CAULKING GUN: a pistol-shaped frame that, loaded with a cylindrical cardboard container of caulking compound, extrudes its contents when a trigger is activated.

CAULKING IRON: a narrow spade-shaped metal instrument (like a chisel with a rounded edge), used with a hammer to drive caulking into a seam.

CENTERBOARD: a short, movable keel lowered and raised from inside a boat, extended through a watertight case to steady the hull and reduce leeway.

CENTERLINE: an imaginary line extended the length of a hull, centered athwartships and parallel to the keel, drawn on boat plans to establish measurements to port and starboard when lofting.

CHINE: hull member of a V-bottom boat where the sides join the bottom; it is fastened to both. Also, the line formed by this jointure.

CLEAT: a device to which a line can be temporarily made fast, usually shaped like a pair of shallow horns.

COAMING: a raised strip of wood erected around a cockpit or other open area to prevent the taking of water.

COTTON WICKING: a rough strand of cotton like thick string, used to caulk a seam.

COUNTERSINK: an oversize pre-boring that permits the head of a fastening to be driven below the surface of any timber; as a verb, to drill or cut such a recess.

CROSS SPALL: a temporary spreader, set athwartships, to keep the sides of a boat in proper relationship until they are permanently fastened.

CROWN: a thwartship convex curve on the upper surface of any exposed portion or member of a hull, sometimes called a camber. A *crowning board* is a device used to define and determine such a curve on any surface for which crown is desired.

CUPPING: the tendency of a board to curve in cross-section, with one side convex and the other concave; produced by the tension of annular rings.

DADO CUTTER: an adjustable group or battery of saw blades, used to cut a wider gap in a piece of wood than that produced by a single blade.

DEADRISE: the angular upward slant of the bottom of a hull from the keel to the turn of the bilge.

DORY: a type of small boat developed by fishermen, noted for its sea-keeping ability. Its narrow transom, called a tombstone, makes it virtually double-ended; it has a narrow, flat bottom, and in its traditional form it is lapstraked.

DOUBLE-ENDED: said of a boat that is sharp at both bow and stern.

DOWEL: a wooden rod available in various small diameters, used as a headless pin to hold two wooden members together.

EDGE-NAILED: said of strip planking, in which each small strake is fastened to the strake below with nails; glue is also used in this type of construction.

EDGE-SET: to drive one carvel plank down on the plank below to achieve wood-to-wood fit despite minor irregularities.

FACE: flat portion of board or construction member.

FAIR: of a curve: flowing, continuous, changing gradually without bumps or flat places.

FLARE: the outreach of sheer beyond beam at waterline.

FLITCH: a plank or thick board cut from a "live" tree, with the bark on.

FLOOR: thwartship structural member across the keel, either alternated with frames or fastened to a frame.

FLOOR BOARDS: boards laid along bottom of boat for walking on.

FLUSH: even with. Chisel bungs, for instance, should be flush with planking.

FRAME: a thwartship member to which planking is fastened; as a verb, to put in frames.

FREEBOARD: height of the sheer above the waterline at any given point along a hull.

GARBOARD: the plank set next to the keel and rabbeted into the keel and stem.

GROMMET: a ring of rope, or a metal eyelet, set in a sail.

GUNWALE: lengthwise strip along sheer of hull (pronounced gunnel).

GUSSET: stiffening bracket between two members that meet each other at right angles or nearly so.

HEEL: of a boat: to lean from the vertical, as to heel over. Also, the lower end of a frame at the keel.

HOOD END: the end of a plank that is buried in the rabbet of the keel or the stem.

JIBE: to change tacks by turning away from the wind, so that the wind crosses the after edge, or leech, of the sail to bear on the other side. Usually accidental, and dangerous if uncontrolled.

JIG: a framework that includes the molds of a boat, so designed as to guide and support the process of assembling a hull. Usually constructed only when a number of hulls are being built to the same design.

JURY RIG: a temporary repair sufficient to permit a boat to reach port.

KEEL: the main structural member of the hull, its backbone, usually extended below the bottom of the hull to steady a boat and provide a "grip" on the water.

KNEE: a strengthening piece that distributes the strain of two angled members and is fastened to both.

KNOT: a rate of speed in terms of nautical miles per hour. (Never say "knots per hour.")

LAPSTRAKE: Planking such that each strake overlaps a portion of the strake below it.

LEE: the side of anything that is away from the wind; leeward (pronounced looard) is in the direction of the lee; a lee shore is to leeward of a boat.

LEEBOARD: similar to a centerboard, but installed outside the hull; a leeboard can be moved to either side, depending on which is the lee.

LEECH: the after edge of a fore-and-aft sail.

LEEWAY: the amount of movement generated when a boat is driven off course to leeward. Current rather than wind can be the cause of sidewise movement.

LIST: a leaning off the vertical, not upright; unlike heeling, listing persists as a result of off-center placement of weight.

LOFT: to lay down the lines of a hull full-size, using a table of offsets (see).

LOOSE-FOOTED: said of a fore-and-aft sail whose foot, or lower edge, is not laced to a boom.

LUFF: forward edge of fore-and-aft sail; as a verb, to head up into the wind.

MAST: a vertical spar, which is the main support of the entire sail rig.

MAUL: a heavy hammer, like a small sledge, usually weighing two to four pounds.

MOLD: the pattern of a thwartship section of a hull, used in construction but not a permanent part of the boat.

106

MOORING: a relatively permanent anchoring system for a boat.

OFFSETS: a tabulated listing of measurements from baseline and centerline to establish points on the elements of a hull shape, by which its lines can be lofted and laid down full-size in preparation for building.

PAINTER: a line made fast to the bow of a small boat, which can be used in temporary tie-ups to a dock or another vessel and when the boat is being towed.

PARTNER: a transverse member of a small boat through which the mast passes to give it bearing at or near the sheerline (see *sheer*).

PAY: obsolete word for caulk.

PEAK: the highest corner of a fore-and-aft sail.

PRE-BORE: to drill holes in wood to receive nails when there is danger of splitting or the wood is too hard for driving nails otherwise. The drill used is a shade smaller than the diameter of the nail. Screws can require pre-boring also.

RABBET: a recess cut into the keel or stem to receive the garboard strake.

RAKE: departure from the vertical; most masts rake aft to a moderate degree.

RIBBAND: light strips of wood—but heavier than battens—set up to follow the shape of a hull as they lie against the molds. They serve to keep the molds steady during the planking process, and each pair of ribbands, port and starboard, are removed as planks are set in their places.

REACH: a sailboat is on a reach when the wind is abeam (at right angles to the keel).

RISER: a horizontal strip on the inside of the hull planking on which the seats, or thwarts, rest.

RUN: the longitudinal curve of the bottom of a hull as it rises toward the stern.

SCARPH: to join two pieces of wood end-to-end or edge-to-edge, both of which must be beveled to permit overlapping with no increase in total thickness. Scarphs are secured with glue; no metal fastenings are used.

SCHOONER: a fore-and-aft rigged vessel with two masts, of which the main or after-mast is the taller. Larger schooners have had from three to seven masts.

SCUPPERS: hole or pipes above the waterline through which water drains overboard.

SEAM: the joint running between two strakes or planks, which is made watertight by caulking.

SEIZE: to bind together or to put a stopper on a line, using small light line.

SHEER: the uppermost line of a hull seen in profile; also called the sheerline. The uppermost strake in a hull is the sheerstrake.

SHEET: the line used to control the position of the sail in relation to the wind. With a boomed sail it is attached to the boom near its outboard end; if the sail is loose-footed, the sheet is attached to the after corner of the sail.

SHIM: to wedge up, or to fill out with thin sheets of metal or other suitable materials.

SHUTTER: the final strake that closes in a hull that has been planked up both from the sheer down and the garboard up.

SLOOP: a fore-and-aft rigged sailboat having only one mast, with one or more headsails forward of the mast. Lacking headsails, it is said to be cat rigged.

SPAR: any shaped timber used to support a sail system, whether mast, boom, gaff, or sprit.

SPILE: to determine and draw the line that defines the shape of the bottom edge of a strake in relation to the top edge of the one below, in carvel planking. This method first transfers measurements from the lower to a batten, and then from the batten to the stock from which the strake above is to be cut.

SPRIT: the light spar which serves to spread a sail by extending one of its corners.

SPRITSAIL: any sail that is set by means of a sprit.

STEAM BOX: a tightly enclosed box designed to accumulate steam and used to render any member of a hull pliable before it is installed.

STEM: the vertical portion of a boat's backbone; it rises from the keel at its forward end.

STEP: of a mast: any construction or device into which the butt end of the mast is set, at the keel. The step and the partner at the sheerline combine to provide stable support of the mast inside the hull.

STRAKE: a single unit of the planking that closes in a boat's hull.

STRIP PLANKING: a method of planking a hull that employs very narrow strakes, usually square in cross-section, each of which is edge-nailed and glued to the strake below.

TACK: to change course by heading a boat into and through the wind to take its pressure on the other side of the sail. When sailing on a tack, a boat is close-hauled or on the wind, as opposed to reaching with the wind abeam, or running before the wind. Also, the lower forward corner of any fore-and-aft sail.

TEMPLATE: a pattern made of wood, paper, or metal from which cut lines can be traced on building stock.

TENDER: of a hull: susceptible to heeling. Also, a small boat used to travel to and from the mooring of a larger one.

THROAT: the uppermost corner of the forward edge of a quadrilateral fore-and-aft sail.

THWART: a seat in a small boat, resting on risers port and starboard.

TRANSOM: the after face of the stern of a boat.

TRIM: the fore-and-aft relationship of a hull in the water; as a verb, to alter a relationship, as in "trim down by the bow," "trim down by the stern," or "trim level."

TRUCK: the uppermost portion of the masthead, opposite of butt.

TUMBLEHOME: the amount by which the sides of a boat's hull curve inward toward the centerline at the sheer.

V-BOTTOM: a boat bottom that is flat throughout the deadrise from keel to chine. So designed, a boat is sometimes described as having a deadrise hull.

WATERLINE: any line of a boat's hull generated by a plane extended parallel to the baseline, or parallel to the boat's load waterline. Specifically, the latter, often designated LWL, is the line at which the hull is designed to float under normal conditions.

WEATHER: toward the wind; the opposite of lee.

WEATHERLY: said of a boat that performs well in adverse conditions of wind and sea.

ZINC: a small plate of that metal attached to a hull below water to divert the eroding effect of electrolysis in salt water to itself and away from functionally essential metal fastening or elements such as the propeller and propeller shaft. Usually, several zincs are placed at strategic points on a powerboat hull, and are replaced after electrolytic action has eaten away more than half their substance.

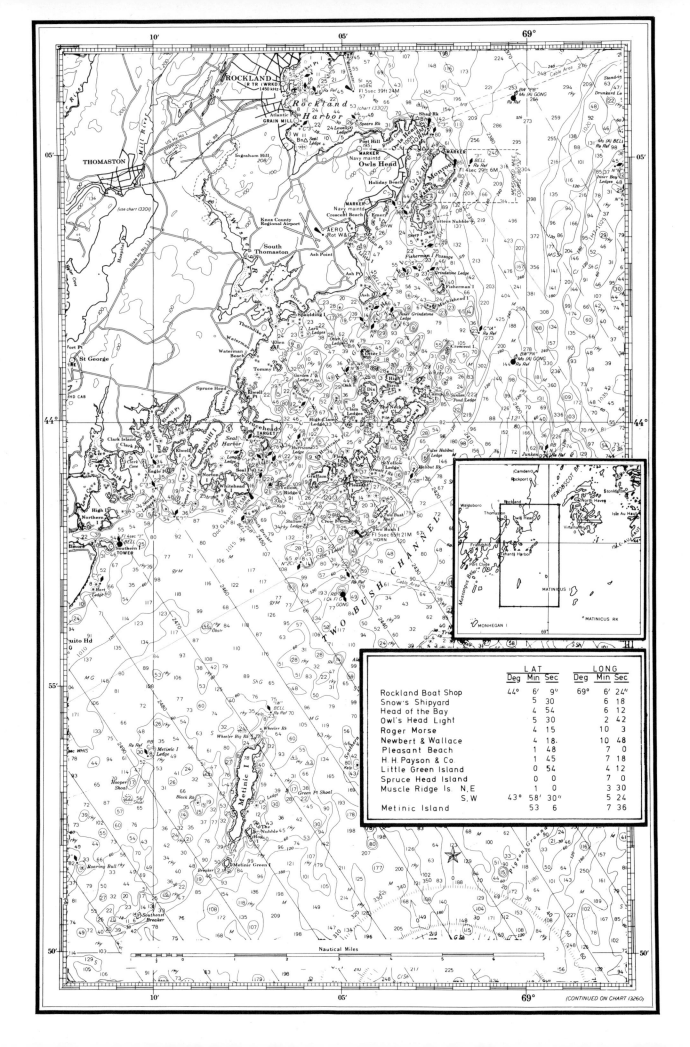

	LAT			LONG		
	Deg	Min	Sec	Deg	Min	Sec
Rockland Boat Shop	44°	6'	9"	69°	6'	24"
Snow's Shipyard		5	30		6	18
Head of the Bay		4	54		6	12
Owl's Head Light		5	30		2	42
Roger Morse		4	15		10	3
Newbert & Wallace		4	18.		10	48
Pleasant Beach		1	48		7	0
H.H. Payson & Co.		1	45		7	18
Little Green Island		0	54		4	12
Spruce Head Island		0	0		7	0
Muscle Ridge Is. N.E		1	0		3	30
S.W	43°	58'	30"		5	24
Metinic Island		53	6		7	36

(CONTINUED ON CHART 13260)

INDEX